D1581708

The Value of Play

Also available from Continuum

The Value of Play

Perry Else

continuum

Continuum International Publishing Group

50 Bedford Square	80 Maiden Lane
London WC1B 3DP	New York NY 10038

www.continuumbooks.com

© Perry Else 2009

First published 2009
Reprinted 2012

All rights reserved. No part of this publication may be reproduced or transmitted in any form or by any means, electronic or mechanical, including photocopying, recording, or any information storage or retrieval system, without prior permission in writing from the publishers.

Perry Else has asserted his right under the Copyright, Designs and Patents Act, 1988, to be identifi ed as Author of this work.

British Library Cataloguing-in-Publication Data
A catalogue record for this book is available from the British Library.

ISBN: 978-0-8264-4809-5 (hardback)
 978-0-8264-9565-5 (paperback)

Library of Congress Cataloging-in-Publication Data
Else, Perry.
The value of play/Perry Else.
 p. cm. Includes bibliographical references.
 ISBN: 978-0-8264-4809-5 (hbk.)
 ISBN: 978-0-8264-9565-5 (pbk.)
1. Play. 2. Early childhood education. 3. Child development. I. Title.
LB1139.35.P55E57 2009
306.4′81–dc22   2008039402

Typeset by Newgen Imaging Systems Pvt Ltd, Chennai, India
Printed and bound in Great Britain

*This book is dedicated with love to
the human beings who taught me
most about the value of play:
Mary, Millie and Ethan.*

Contents

Acknowledgements

Thank you to my friends and relations who helped by sharing their experiences and answering my awkward questions: Rita and Paddy, Eileen and Derek, Barbara and Alan, Julia and Eloise, Ali, Andy, Gertie, and The Cohen/Blackmore, Coyne/Baggaley, Else, Knowles, McKenna and Moran-Healy Families.

For their permission to use their images in my photos I'm grateful to Ariana, Chai, Charlie, Eddie, Ethan, George, Grace, Jess, Kish, Millie, Roseanne, Sam, William and Zakah.

Thanks to all the people who attended and supported the *Beauty of Play* Conferences, showing that it's good for adults to play.

Thanks to Bob Hughes for showing where the treasure was buried and Gordon Sturrock for giving me a compass and a spade.

Introduction

The tide retreats and the sand is left clean and smooth, ready for the day ahead. The first families arrive and start claiming plots of sand with towels, beach shelters and wind-breaks. Some children, covered in sun-cream begin wandering around, exploring this new environment with fingers and sticks. Smaller children will discover the sand and stones, toddlers will move around, feeling the new sensations on their feet and hands. Some will use their hands or spades to create miniature worlds that will be populated with feathers, sticks or imaginations. Two or three games of beach cricket or football start up, each with their own rules and oddly sized team members, with mums and dads from time to time taking sides or acting as umpire. The children shriek and shout but no-one tells them off or to 'be quiet' – the beach seems to be big enough to hold whatever it is the children need to do. Later on, as they begin to extend their range, the children explore tide pools, looking for crabs and starfish. Older children create mounds and trenches, some of which go all the way to the sea. The wind raises a few breakers so the more adventurous put on wet suits to go bodyboarding or swimming. Wandering by the sea, one child gets lost but is shepherded back to her family by another mother. As the wind picks up, kites begin dancing in the air, bothering the seagulls flying by. When the tide turns, the sun begins falling into the horizon and some groups pack up and reluctantly trudge away. Others put on their T-shirts and light up barbecues. The children play with the flames and take a branch to make a fire of their own. Everyone dines on the scorched food, it tasting better for the sharing and open air. Someone tells a story and a round begins, ending with a song and laughter. As the tide begins to tickle toes, everyone rushes to tidy up in the dark and get back to the dunes before all is washed away. Once again the sand is left clean and smooth, ready for the day ahead.

Figure 0.1 Endless possibilities on the beach

On the beach, we don't need reminding about the value of play – it's all there before us. Children (and adults) generally doing what they want when they want to do it – free to start and stop as the mood takes them. Along the way finding out what it is to be human and alive, what the environment supports and what we can do in it and what our neighbours can do with and for us. It's a world of creation and destruction, of stillness and constant motion, satisfaction and frustration, happiness and occasional sadness. It's far away from the 'normal' world of rules and timetables but people are busy none the less; busy being alive and experiencing it all.

> We often contrast 'play' behaviour with 'serious' behaviour, but perhaps the truth is that we would be better off treating play as the most serious aspect of all our activities. (Desmond Morris 1977 p. 270)

What will be covered in this book

'Play' is an interesting phenomenon; it represents what is most fleeting in our lives, the moments of play that pass and are gone – yet childhood memories of play may also be the most valuable and treasured as we grow older. For every definition of play, there are arguments in support and others that contradict – the value of play is hard to capture. In the following chapters a number of perspectives are taken to explore the meanings of play and how it might be valuable to children, to adults and to government and the wider community.

We start with trying to say what we mean by play in Chapter 1. The definition used in this book follows that generally used in the UK: playing children choose the content and purpose of their actions, following their own instincts, ideas and interests, in their own way for their own reasons. We know that children can play by themselves without any adult support; the desire to play comes from within. An argument is made to help understand how the *play process* works and how adults may be both a resource and a barrier for children's play.

In Chapter 2 we look at what gets in the way of children playing. Parents and adults working with children know that playing is good for children but are often confused by the dangers they see in the wider environment and so may restrict children's natural opportunities to play. A number of possible barriers are explained and there is a brief summary of legislation impacting on children's play.

'Why is play valuable' is the theme of the next chapter. The need for children to take risks both physically and emotionally is explained in relation to the play drive and human development and survival. Yet play is also about 'now' and how children become immersed in play to forget all other needs. The varieties and extremes of play are discussed to try to arrive at a balanced point of view. Despite what some in our society think, we can never exclusively be in the objective world of facts and figures, and there is always the human waiting to comment and express feelings about what it has experienced. A model that draws together all these differing views on the purpose of play is presented and the different types of play are explained: these ideas are then used as the basis for the remaining chapters of the book: why playing is valuable to our bodies, our minds, culturally and socially.

Chapter 4, 'Playing actively' looks at why children need to be active and especially so outdoors. The argument is made that children be given the space and freedom to play from an early age. It's clear that the quality of the environment affects children as the better the quality of that environment, the better the opportunities for play. Adults control environments so can influence them for the better, both at home and elsewhere.

From before they are born, children are able to perceive the world around them, so the topic of Chapter 5 is 'Playing through feelings and thoughts'. The value of such play is discussed with some reference to brain development. Though the focus is on the internal world, the impact of the wider environment is also discussed as the key influences on children are many and varied; their development and well-being is integral with their surroundings and those who share it. This leads on to how we relate to others, the theme of Chapter 6.

Children's play is influenced by cultural elements whether they are subtle or obvious; it is increasingly recognized that they construct their own view of the world and explore things in their play that some adults might disapprove of. Adult attitudes whether conscious or not are often what restrict children's play the most. The different forms of cultural play are explained with some examples.

Some societies believe in playing with their children, others do so in varying degrees and this is discussed in Chapter 7. Yet social play is essential to children's interactions with others and adults need to be sensitive to intervening in children's play. Much of modern childhood is defined by relationships to others, either in real or virtual worlds. Through playing with others, children find out about negotiation and compromise, about leading and following – and about the absence of rules. The relationship between girls and boys in their play is looked at, as is the 'darker side' of social play. The argument for the participation of children in service development is presented, recognizing that some adults find it challenging to include children's opinions in decision making.

Play is continually creative and can carry on endlessly and this is the subject of the chapter on 'Grown-up play'. Examples of adult forms of play are listed and the different manifestations of play for artists, scientists, writers and philosophers are described. The challenge is offered to remain playful throughout life.

Chapter 9 gives a history of play from early times to the modern day, with a brief outline of key ideas and theorists from the broad field of human development and children's play.

The last chapter looks at the *Every Child Matters* framework in England and how playwork is expected to contribute to the five outcomes. Children's play has gained increased awareness among a variety of professions working with children, many of whom have different approaches to playing and children. The challenge for settings is therefore to provide an environment that supports play to meet the child's needs and attempts to meet the five outcomes.

The text is illustrated throughout with examples from observations of playing children to help explain the process under discussion. Key questions are asked at times to help those who may be studying or interested in a more reflective form of practice. And there are anecdotes from a number of people who enjoyed their childhood some years ago. These were collected as original research for this publication and are used to highlight some of the changes that have taken place in the past three generations. The form and opportunities for children's play have and continue to change; whether for the better you will need to form your own opinion based on what follows. We start off by looking at what is meant by 'play'.

1

What do we mean by play?

Play is what I do when everyone else has stopped telling me what to do.

   Sometimes I like to make stuff, sometimes I like to play games, sometimes I like messing about, sometimes I don't like doing anything.

Anonymous children[1]

It is in playing and only in playing that the individual child or adult is able to be creative and to use the whole personality, and it is only in being creative that the individual discovers the self.

D. W. Winnicott[2]

Play is the highest form of research.

Albert Einstein

We've all seen very young children lost in playing, where everything that happens is a joy and a surprise. Think of toddlers walking for the first time – it's hard, a challenge and it can hurt if they get it wrong – but when they get it right, we see their faces light up with spontaneous pleasure. Or what about a young child playing by themselves, chatting away to a not-quite-imaginary friend about what they were doing that day. They will be playing with feelings and friendships to see how things work. And the teenager trying on the third outfit before going out on the town, their behaviour may be different but they are playing with independence and individuality – finding out who they are, as is the young child who is talking to their imaginary friend.

Defining play

Play may be a paradox to theorists, but to good friends, it's a sure thing.[3]

Everyone knows what play is; we've all done it and we see it all around us. But ask anyone to say what 'play' is and we often have a problem. Play has many sides and many characters; due to its nature, a definition of play is hard to pin down. For some people, it's simple – play is not work; it's what we do for fun, to wind down and relax, and when we don't have something else to do. For teachers, play is how young children learn; for coaches it's the way we start to keep fit; for neighbours it is how we first find out about one another. For other people it's more serious than work; when we are playing is when we are most alive, most truly ourselves. A clue to what unites all these points of view is given in the opening quote above; play is often what we choose to do for ourselves when we want to do it – when no-one else is telling us what to do. Play is often described as behaviour that is led by the individual because they want to do it; it is freely chosen activity that is carried out for the 'pleasure' of it. Play can be pleasurable but it can also be satisfying, fun, frustrating, challenging, scary, risky, empowering, alienating, zany – and when we feel most alive.

More than 'just behaviour', play – or more accurately – *playing* – is a *process*; one that is flexible, inquisitive and creative. We play because we want to experience more, feel more, think more and we want to be challenged or we will be 'bored'. In play there is always an element of surprise or risk that sets the experience apart from the routine of life.

With the pleasure we get from playing comes the powerful urge or drive to repeat playful activities; and the more children play, the better they become at it and so learn control over themselves and their environment – vital skills if they are to survive in the world. But more than just survival, playing helps

Play is a natural instinct which we do because we enjoy it, we learn from it and it stops us from being bored.

children gain a sense of control with an accompanying sense of success and confidence. With young children it is very easy to see the process taking place and to link playing with growth and development as many theorists have done.[4] In this context many people see play as vital for human development; children need to play so that they can learn to become fully human.

> **Key questions**
>
> - How did you play as a child?
> - Where did you play? Inside or out?
> - Who did you play with? Sisters, brothers, friends?
> - Where were the adults?
>
> Make notes and reflect on them as you read on.

Playing – just for children?

Children and people of all ages play, but as we grow older, playing becomes more organized and we may need to look harder to see the signs. By and large, children explore the world as toddlers, learn to get on with other people as preschoolers, find out about themselves and their way of doing things in primary school and then start becoming independent before becoming adults at the end of secondary school.

The business of playing is important for children's longer term development and their learning, but also for their sense of self, health and well-being and their relationships with others. As children grow, playing can involve thoughts and feelings, fantasy and creativity, friendships and communities, as well as physical activity. All these experiences contribute to their physical, emotional and social well-being. Play is so effective because it helps children and young people to 'know' through experience, not by being told by someone else. Exerting this choice is crucial to helping us become more ourselves, learning from our mistakes in our own ways and to the best of our knowledge and ability.

The trouble is, when we grow up we become serious, rational and logical, and we start to think that children and young people's play is not important because it looks frivolous, irrational, 'just playing'. We give much more priority to our own adult concerns; things like cars, buildings, commerce, protecting private land and so on. We also think that children and young people should spend

Play is a process of continuing learning + development which enriches or health + well being.

Figure 1.1 'Just playing' – fun or fundamental?

their time doing more 'worthwhile' activities such as formal, structured learning, organized activities or sports. Play becomes 'frivolous' – something to be saved for our spare time, our 'play time'. In the increasingly market-led economy that we call society in the West, the pressure on children and young people to be responsible and make an economic contribution leads to parents and other adults expecting more work from children and this leaves less time for play.

Example: What did play mean to us as children?

As part of an area play strategy for an inner-city area of Sheffield, UK a mixed group of participants aged '25–65' were asked what they used to play as children. These are some of the things they came up with:

- 'It', 'Tiggy' or Tag – a chasing game where someone is 'on' or 'it', he or she has to chase, then touch, another player who then becomes 'it'
- Tiggy chain – a chasing game where those who are caught have to hold hands to catch the others

⇨

As we get older we see play as frivolous + think children should be involved in more formal structured play. Children have less time to play due to societal pressures.

Example—cont'd

- 'Kick the can' – a running and racing game with a tin can as base
- Hop scotch – a hopping game on a chalk pattern
- French skipping – skipping over elasticated strings (a big version of 'cat's cradle')
- 'Cops and robbers', 'Cowboys and Indians' – dramatic hide and chase games
- Imaginary games – pretending, for example, doctors and nurses, greengrocers, captain of an island
- Skipping with a tennis ball in a long stocking
- French cricket – where the batter's legs are the stumps
- Spinning a tin can with a fire in it (!)
- Kiss Chase – does it need an explanation?
- Roller skating
- Hide and seek
- Country games – blowing grass, making lace from bracken
- Improvised, made up ball games
- Football
- Dressing up
- Making things – *papier maché*, mobiles, painting boxes, rose petal scent
- Cat's Cradle – a string knotting game, usually between pairs
- Jigsaw puzzles
- Sewing and knitting, French knitting – crochet
- Cooking sweets and little cakes
- Mischievous games – being naughty, knocking on doors and running away
- Playing in gangs – out in the street at all hours
- Fishing with bamboo canes and little nets for 'stickle backs' in local streams
- Making balsa wood gliders – and flying them off the top of hills
- 'Delavio' – a chase game where once found, 'it' must hold the other, and say '1, 2, 3, 4, 5, 6, 7, 8, 9, 10 Delavio' before they get away; if caught they join 'it'
- 'Film stars' – for others to guess who you are, a version of the party game Charades
- Rolling down a grassy hill
- Paper games – noughts and crosses, 'hangman' etc.
- Playing with names and the letters in your name – usually rhymes and teases or predicting the future
- Swinging – on playgrounds and from trees
- Board games, marbles, tiddlywinks, jacks
- Train sets
- Toy car games – 'Dinky' toys
- Getting dizzy; by spinning around

- Adventures on bikes with provisions and sweets
- 'Dare' games – daring others to do 'naughty' things
- Catapults – which were used to hit people sometimes!
- Feeding ducks and squirrels
- Grass games in fields – flattening down areas and looking up to the sky; 'grass angels'
- Old fashioned toys – kite flying, hoops, spinning tops.

A definition of play

We all played as children, and we can see play in the young of other animal species as well; just as cats play to learn hunting skills, humans play to learn survival skills (as well as cultural and political skills). We can presume that playing serves some basic biological purpose. Nature has given children a 'drive to play' for a reason that has something to do with survival. This makes playing fundamentally important and something that we should support – we will return to these arguments later in the chapter on the importance of play, 'Why is play valuable'.

For now, let's review the definition of play:[5]

- Play is a process – it's the way of playing that is important; not what we play with
- Play is freely chosen by the player – a child tidying up the garden because her mum told her to is not playing
- Play is personally directed; the manner of playing is decided by the child – tidying up the garden might change into play if the child enjoys exploring the feel of mud under her feet, or the sound of the leaves being piled up
- Play is engaged in for its own sake; the impulse comes from within – the child must find the activity satisfying and derive pleasure from it – which might cause conflict with any adult ideas (playing with mud will not get the garden tidy!).

There are many actions that may not start out as play but become playful as the people involved play with different aspects of the experience. Activities may start out led by others but only become playful when the player wants them to be, when they engage with the action for their own reasons. In summary, playing children choose the content and purpose of their actions, following their own instincts, ideas and interests, in their own way for their own reasons.

This understanding has implications for how we support playing. Children will often begin playing for their own reasons with whatever comes to hand, in whatever kind of environment; sometimes this will be fine, other times, adults may find it inconvenient or just plain 'wrong'. Examples would be the child playing with food; at home in their high chair, it might be seen by parents as playful and funny. But in another's house or at a special occasion like a wedding, it may be embarrassing to the adult and therefore 'wrong' for that time. At other times, we may try to support playing by taking the child to a playground or by starting a special activity such as cooking. If the child is curious and in a playful mood then they will join in, but if the child is tired or distracted by something else, they will not be playing and the adult may feel frustrated. With the best intentions, we may try to lead the play, but if the children do not want to play, there is little we can do about it. The best we can do is to create a playful environment for children and understand that playing will start and stop of its own accord. We may try and support that process but should not be surprised if the playing takes off on a life of its own that leaves us behind.

> ## Key questions
>
> Think about what has been said and then answer these questions:
>
> - What does 'play' mean for you?
> - What was your favourite play activity?
> - What did you think you got from your play?

The play process

To support playing, we need to understand how the *play process* works and so how sometimes we can be a resource and other times a barrier for children's play. We know that children – even from very young ages – can play by themselves without any adult support; the desire to play comes from within and they play with the environment in which they find themselves as shown above. Let's explore some of the scenes that were presented above.

Think of a toddler playing with their food; they are clearly not being taught how to eat, the 'game' is an active process whereby the child tries out various actions to see what works and what happens. As far as we know, there is no rational thought in the toddler's head that says 'do this' or 'try that' – the child is 'just doing it' for the pleasure and satisfaction they get from the activity. Looking at the activity in more detail, we see that the child tries one thing, sees what happens then tries another. An observation of a child in a high chair shows that she first eats the food as well as she is able; this may be with a spoon but is more often with her bare hands. The sensation of sauce on her face becomes pleasurable so she plays with that and smears the sauce all over her face, then her arms and finally the food tray in front of her. She then notices that the sauce leaves patterns on the tray surface that can be changed and altered by the applications of fingers and hands on the tray. 'Trapped' in the high chair, the child plays with the sauce till it becomes cold and congeals, then she tries to move out of the chair and offers a few squeals to let her father know that she wants to be moved. What started out as a game related to survival (eating) became a sensory and then an embryonic artistic activity, before needing rudimentary communication to move to another game. The child's playing was constrained (but not stopped) by being strapped into the high chair and the resources available on that chair.

This observation can be simply described in reference to the *play cycle*[6] as follows:

- The toddler has a desire to play, which we see in the 'play cue', the expressed intention to play, which may be an action, a visual cue, a touch or a spoken cue – in this case it was the interaction with the sauce
- The environment in which the play takes place, the 'play frame' – in this example the high chair and the available resources
- The 'play return' in this case is environmental, though it may come from another person – the sensory and visual experience of playing with the sauce
- The child's response, which may be active, passive or non-existent – in this case it is active, exploring the various qualities of the sauce and the environment.

The start to the play process comes from within, with a desire to play. While we don't know what starts this drive to play, nor what shifts the 'normal' activity into a playful one, we can recognize the playful cues which show that 'this is play'. These clues that playing has started include obvious physical actions that especially in young children are often repetitive or exaggerated, spoken cues such as clear invitations or playful sounds and subtle body language (smiles, eyebrow raises, flamboyant gestures). Let's use an example from an older child, playing with a sand tray and a varied

PLAY CYCLE :
desire to play → play cue
Environment → play frame
Experience → play return

collection of toys. The child starts by exploring the qualities of the sand – children learn from an early age that sand has many different qualities depending on the nature of the sand particles and the amount of water held by the sand. Sand is best for modelling when it is neither too dry nor too wet. The cues that the child is playing include gentle stoking movements in the sand to assess its quality and occasional mumbles to himself about the play possibilities and options. When he wants someone else to join him he may offer a spoken request, though usually the cue will not be vocalized and will be made up of intimate actions that subtly tell the other that it's ok to join in. These actions include playing towards the other's space, leaving a toy in their corner and making regular eye contact to check that each is aware of the other.

The 'play frame' is the space, the environment in which the play takes place. With the boy playing with a sand tray, it is easy to see the play as contained by the tray, but the play space also includes the space occupied by the playing child and what they are thinking and doing. The cues may also be offered to other children around the tray who may be close by the tray or quite distant from it. The physical space of the tray supports the playing but the play is not limited to the tray. This becomes clear when the boy takes handfuls of sand and places them on the floor to make patterns on the flat surface.

Like in the high chair example, a child making patterns in the sand is getting sufficient 'return' from the playful activity to not need the support of another. But often in play, the play return is more dynamic and interactive. When the sand tray boy offers a toy to another child, she takes the toy and offers a return (her own play cue) into the play space. He responds gently at first, checking out the nature of the game. A modelling and building game begins where the children start creating their own town to be peopled by the toys available and the imaginary beings they co-create. Like the play cue, the play return from another may be spoken, visual or by use of their body. And like all repetitions of the play cycle, the playing child may choose to engage or not with that return.

By responding to the play return, the child maintains, extends or stops the developing play cycle. Quite often in the early stages of playing together, children will try different play forms till an unspoken compromise is reached and the play proper begins. Maintenance of the play cycle can be seen as passive, where neither player wants to upset the game by taking it in

Figure 1.2 Playing with sand and water

new directions. In the sand tray, children will often respect each other's creations, knowing that to be too active will often demolish the other's work. Active extension of the play may disrupt the form of play being enjoyed in order to create another form. Introducing water to the sand tray may at first make a 'mess' in the dry sand but it will facilitate more accurate and distinctive modelling of the material. And when the play has finished for one child, she signals by walking out of the play frame, ending that form for herself without affecting the other. At another time, she may signal that she wants to do something different by deliberately obliterating the play forms she has carefully built in the sand. Adults watching can often be dismayed by this action, but for the child the playing has finished; they got whatever they needed from the process; they have no need of the product of their play. This 'annihilation'[7] is often seen not just in the sand tray but also in the bigger play space of the beach where twice a day, the tide comes in to wipe clean the playing field. Children are aware of this and often build castles and small towns close to the water's edge, taking pleasure from the gradual destruction of their creations.

PLAY ANNIHILATION → play is ended by child and they move on

> ## Activity: Looking for play cues
>
> Observe a group of children playing.
>
> - Can you see the play cues firing off from one to the other? How often are they repeated? How often do they change?
> - What do you think is the play frame? Is it determined by the environment or by the children? How often does it change?
> - When does play change or end? Whose decision was it?

The play cycle suggests both the repetitive and developing nature of play and it also shows that the process can be disrupted if any of the elements are missing. The child can choose to play the same game over and over again while ever they are getting what they need from that action. They can also adapt, extend or stop the cycle in response to the return by changing the play frame or by issuing cues in different manners. We will return to the elements of the play cycle in many examples in later pages.

Notes

1. The introductory quote from an anonymous child comes from Cole-Hamilton and others (2002) *Making the Case for Play – Gathering the Evidence*. This report on the benefits of play contains many similarly astute comments from children.
2. DW Winnicott (1971) *Playing and Reality* London: Penguin p. 63.
3. This is attributed 'after Trevarthen' in Brian Sutton-Smith (1997) *The Ambiguity of Play* London: Harvard University Press p. 127.
4. We will look at the various theorists who commented about play in Chapter 9.
5. There are many definitions of play around, though the key terms in this list of elements are based on the work of Bob Hughes and Frank King as quoted in *Best Play* (2000) London: NPFA/ Children's Play Council/Playlink.
6. Gordon Sturrock and Perry Else (1998) 'The playground as therapeutic space: playwork as healing' – also known as 'The Colorado Paper', in *Therapeutic Playwork Reader One* (2005) Southampton: Common Threads.

   The play cycle as described was first set down by Gordon Sturrock and Perry Else (1998) though others have used similar concepts in describing what happens in play. For example, 'cues' as described by Brian Sutton-Smith and Diana Kelly-Byrne (1984) The idealization of play, in Peter K Smith (Ed.) *Play in Animals and Humans* Oxford: Blackwell; and 'frames' by Gregory Bateson (1973) *Steps to an Ecology of Mind* New York: Chandler Publishing Company.

7. 'Annihilation' and other terms from the play cycle are discussed extensively in 'The Colorado Paper', Gordon Sturrock and Perry Else (1998) as quoted earlier.

2 What gets in the way of children playing?

Alan was talking about the difference between his own childhood in the middle of the twentieth century and that of children in the twenty-first:

> I feel a bit sorry for kids these days; they can't play like we used when we were younger. There are pressures on them that there shouldn't be, the values and interests are so different. But I still think that if they were given the opportunity to play in the rivers and swing off trees they'd be doing it.
>
> We should try to get kids talking more to each other and their neighbours and to do that I'd limit TV to two hours a day, computers to one; I'd get rid of all celebrities, ban mobile phones, and ration the use of cars.

Of course we cannot turn the clock back and childhood now is very different to what it was fifty, thirty or even ten years ago – each child has a different set of circumstances in which they grow up, but there are many features of what Alan says that are shared by people who understand how children play; we'll explore those in the following section.

Many people have strong opinions about children and childhood:

'Children have no responsibilities these days, they have no respect'
'It's the problem of the parents; they should be firmer'
'The police should patrol more'
'The Council should provide more after school and youth clubs'

…and so it goes on. The truth is that children live (as do we all) in a world that has many influences upon it; but children often have less influence than adults and so are affected by the decisions that adults make on their behalf. Children's desires and needs are crucial to what they do and how they play, but they are influenced by friends and family, by legislation in the wider community and through the media by the celebrities that Alan wants to get rid of. As much as we might challenge it, our individual views and opportunities are shaped and constrained by those of people, cultures and governments around us and by the physical environment in which we live. How the wider world 'contaminates' children's play environments is explored in the following pages.

The wider world contaminates the play environment

Key questions

Before you read this chapter, answer these questions for yourself:

- What stops children from playing?
- Make a list of the things you can think of.
- Add to your list as you read through this chapter.

Family and friends

Despite rumours to the contrary the adults closest to children, their parents, still have a big influence in children's lives; most crucially in the first eight years but really until children leave home. What parents believe and more critically how they act influences children as they are growing up. We've all seen girls who are 'just like their mum' and boys who are a 'chip off the old block'. Parents as well as passing on their genes and physical characteristics to their offspring also pass on their culture and beliefs, either consciously or accidentally.

Parents still biggest influence.

'Hyper-parenting' is the term used to describe the practice of parents who believe that they and they alone can control the destiny of their little ones. Children are often guarded from external influences, schools will be chosen, after school classes booked and holiday camps organized. Hyper-parents may also book children into development classes before they are born, use 'flash cards' of text or numbers to stimulate their children from very early ages, who fill every waking moment of the child's life with 'stimulating and interesting' activities, be these music or maths, dance or drama. Whether every child turns out to be gifted in the chosen area has yet to be proven, but what is clear is that children will have little time to be truly themselves in these 'hot house', claustrophobic environments. Increasingly we see the results of this approach to child rearing in precocious children who don't know how to make friends and play with their peers as they have never been more than a few hours in the company of children outside their family.

The influence of 'laid back' parents while not as explicit is just as strong; if we leave things to chance in our children's lives, they are just as likely to follow that pattern for themselves and grow up to believe that 'what happens will happen'. Parents feel that children are 'free' to develop whatever interests they choose, but of course those interests are influenced by what is close to hand and familiar. While recognizing that all children will have different life experiences, it is common to see children who are 'obsessed' with one thing or another to the exclusion of all else. Those children will only play with what they know and feel comfortable with; stereotypically, girls following fashion and pop music, and boys football. These children can often be very confident – indeed overconfident – with what is familiar, but resistant to experience new activities or new situations.

Of course most parents will be somewhere in between these extremes; each with their own way of trying to give their child the best start possible. Fortunately the number of parents who deliberately set out to hold back or damage their child in some way is rare. Most parents do the best they can for their children based on the knowledge and information they have up to that point in their lives. Some will be good with physical activities and doing things, other will be better at relationships and feelings; some will be good at 'head' stuff, working things out or planning. It's rare for anyone to be good at everything. It is all a question of balance; children who have access to a wide range of play opportunities and variety in their environment will tend to have a broad range of play experiences and will tend to be confident across that range. We will explore this in Chapter 3.

Legislation impacting on children

Whatever parents feel about raising their children; it is clear that a huge change has occurred in child care habits in the past 30 years. In the 1970s many children in the UK were 'latch key' children; with their own key to the family home, letting themselves in and out while parents were out at work. Concerns about the safety of children and fears of what they might be up to lead to calls for the provision of child care for working parents and those in training schemes. This has followed a trend of increasing concern for the welfare of children going back well over 100 years in the UK (with slight variations across England, Scotland, Wales and Northern Ireland).

In 1889, the 'children's charter' as it was known, gave police the power to enter homes if it was suspected that children were being abused.[1] The first Children Act was published in 1908 and introduced the registration of foster parents. Subsequent improvements in the relevant acts brought together all existing child protection law, lead to supervision orders for children at risk, and then established a children's committee and a children's officer in each local authority. In 1970, social services departments were created to look after children's safety, health and welfare. The Children Act 1989 gave every child the right to protection from abuse and exploitation. It made law the belief that children are usually best looked after within their family.

In 2003, the *Every Child Matters* Green Paper said that children's trusts should be set up with a children's director overseeing local services that amalgamated health, education and social services. Later additions led to The Children Act 2004 which covered the universal services that every child may need with more targeted services for those with additional needs. The overall aim of The Children Act 2004 was to encourage integrated planning, commissioning and delivery of services. It also aimed to improve multidisciplinary working, remove duplication, increase accountability and improve the coordination of inspections in local authorities. In support of this legislation, the UK Government's Ten Year Strategy for Childcare, *Choice for parents, the best start for children*, was published in December 2004. A strategy with a broad remit, it set targets that by 2010 free part-time early education places for 3- and 4-year-olds would be extended to 20 hours a week, 3,500 children's centres were to be established to provide access for all families and all 5- to 11-year-olds would access affordable school-based childcare all year round. In brief, the legislation was to lead to a situation where all children from 3 to 11 years would be cared for in children's centres and schools for much of the school year. However, the 12-week school holiday periods were still under resourced and ad hoc arrangements for care resulted in children being left with friends, family and neighbours or reverting to 'latch key' arrangements, where they effectively cared for themselves.

Overall, the increased provision of child care combined with the increased integration of women into the formal workforce and the extension of the working week from six days to seven resulted in changes in perceptions about child care and child safety among parents. These changes (influenced by government policy and the media) led to many parents feeling that children needed to be cared for and instructed in what to do in their spare time. Parents were fearful because some no longer believed that children were capable of looking after themselves and were also concerned in case they (the parents) should be accused of child abuse or child neglect by leaving children alone. These fears resulted in changed behaviour towards children's freedom and ability to play out. One of the key influencers in the way that parents view children's safety has been the media.

Influences of the media

While newspaper and glossy magazines still play a role, TV makes the biggest influence in the lives of young people and their families. More than half of Western 3-year-olds have a TV set in their bedrooms.[2] According to the Broadcasters' Audience Research Board, the average 6-year-old will have watched TV for around one full year of their lives[3] and the figure is likely to be higher for children from homes where parents are in lower paid employment. Research on American children suggests that by the age of 12 they will have seen over 200,000 TV adverts. Watching television occupies the majority of the Western world's leisure time, taking up more waking time than any other single activity except work. The consequences of this change in human habits have raised many concerns among biologists and psychologists. The influence of TV is considered to be a key factor in the increase in childhood obesity, the rate of children diagnosed as having attention disorders, the growth in the belief of shopping as a way of living and in the earlier 'adultification' of children, with them borrowing the clothes, mannerisms and attitudes of the celebrity adults seen on TV. Media messages also affect parents and their perceptions of childhood.

Activity: Messages in the media

Make an effort to look at the content of TV reporting about children, or collect news-papers over a week and note the key stories.

- What are the main stories about?
- How are children and young people represented?
- How positive or negative are the stories?
- Who speaks for the children?

Why are playgrounds so boring these days? Don't they realize that older children like to play as well?

Gertie

Over the past 20 years, children's outdoor play experiences in the UK have been influenced by a campaign originally started by the BBC's *That's Life!* pro-gramme. This programme as well as being entertaining, was one of the early TV consumer 'champions' that became common in the UK (e.g. *Watchdog, Rogue Traders, House of Horrors*). Following an incident where a child had died as a result of an accident on a playground, the programme – with good intentions – argued and campaigned for 'safety surfacing' to be installed in public playgrounds. Understandably (it is always a tragedy when a child loses their life) this campaign was successful and reflected the mood of recent years, where consumers felt that if something had gone wrong, it was not an 'acci-dent' but that someone or something was to blame. Local authorities came under much pressure to 'upgrade' their playgrounds, in many cases removing play equipment and installing safety surfaces. Spaces that had been informally used for play were dismantled and lost to several generations of children.

At a play conference in the UK in 2006,[4] it was reported that the market in safety surfaces had risen to around £50 million per annum, or around a third of what is spent on public play spaces each year. However this spend was in contradiction to the advice of the Health & Safety Executive (HSE). In 2002, the HSE Report 426[5] stated that there was no evidence that safety surfaces had affected the incidence of injuries in playground accident statis-tics for the decade from 1988. Fortunately, the rate of deaths from accidents on playgrounds had been low at around one every four years; the analysis was therefore based on visits to hospital resulting from playground falls. In a comparison of different surfaces, a natural grass surface appeared safer than other common play ground surfaces; therefore as a whole, the UK play industry is spending £50 million a year on safety surfacing, a product that does not seem to produce any significant play or safety benefits.

As well as the drive for 'safe' playgrounds, we have 'stranger danger', where everyone who is not a family member is seen as a predator waiting to abduct or abuse children as they wander through the environment. Whereas two generations ago, neighbours and strangers were seen as 'good Samaritans', they are now seen as potential criminals, with many people fearful of helping children in case their actions are misconstrued. Again the media have contributed to the fears of parents and children by reporting high profile cases in a sensationalist way. Horrendous though the stories of child murderer Mary Bell, victim Jamie Bulger and the Soham murderer Ian Huntley may be, they are still very rare. By far the highest incidences of abuse and harm are caused by those closest to children in their immediate circle of friends and family.[6] The mismatch between fears and reality may be added to with the change in our home and work habits. As more households have parents in work there is less time to be 'neighbourly'; more people are racing from home to work to leisure activity, usually in their car – which of course is another major barrier to playing out.

Concerns with 'safety'

We used to go for long walks; we'd take a bottle of water, and some jam sandwiches and we used to walk for miles which you could do in those days… We'd paddle in the local stream, we collected flowers and sit in the grass; people would say 'Hello' and you were not frightened.

Eileen

These misperceptions of what constitutes 'safe' have severely impacted on children's playing experiences. We now have what writer Tim Gill calls a 'zero risk childhood',[7] one that has affected how we regard childhood in the twenty-first century. This perspective has led us to limit childhood experience and so the development of children's autonomy, resilience and sense of responsibility. Gill believes that children in the UK are so controlled and supervised that 'they have very little idea of how the wider world works, and either go wild or struggle to cope'. People working with young offenders have reported that many had spent their lives watching television or hanging round estates and had never played outside. We see the results of this in media reports with more children being given 'ASBOs' (Anti-Social Behaviour Orders). We also have the phenomenon of children being treated as if they need to be wrapped in cotton wool. In February 2007, a primary school near Lincoln banned the games of Tag and Kiss Chase because staff felt playtime was becoming too rough and a school in Buckinghamshire stopped lunchtime kickabouts in case passers-by were hit by a football. A school in Sheffield instructed parents that children would no longer be allowed to touch others during 'playtime' – at a stroke, innocent games of tag were outlawed. Teachers at other schools reacting to safety fears have also banned conkers and snowball fights and have even closed schools in snowy weather because of fears that pupils and staff might fall.

While the issues are complex, overall what we are seeing is a reduction in the opportunity for children to be children and to play freely. Many people feel we need a concerted effort to change attitudes to childhood safety. Serious steps have been taken in this direction by some agencies. These issues will not be fully explored here other than to report on some of the work being done to help the wider society understand the importance of play and risk in children's lives.

Children need to take risks

Most of the things we played would be considered dangerous: walking along the tops of walls was a favourite pastime. If you couldn't walk along the top of a wall that was five feet high then you were a bit of a ninny.

Derek

The Play Safety Forum (an independent body which brings together the main national organizations with an interest in safety and children's play) has issued a statement about managing risk in provision for play. While recognizing that risk assessment involves making complex judgements that balance benefits and risks, the Play Safety Forum says this about children and risk:

All children both need and want to take risks in order to explore limits, venture into new experiences and develop their capacities, from a very young age and from their earliest play experiences. Children would never learn to walk, climb stairs or ride a bicycle unless they were strongly motivated to respond to challenges involving a risk of injury.[8]

The statement is limited to provision that is designed to meet children's play needs, usually play equipment and play grounds, but the message is relevant to children's play in the wider world. The statement concludes by saying that

Figure 2.1 Walking along the tops of walls

if children do not find the provision exciting and attractive, it will fail them by not meeting their playing needs.

The concern with 'safety' is also addressed in the Health & Safety Executive (HSE) Report 426 where author Prof. David Ball says: 'perhaps [the term "safety" is] best avoided altogether, particularly in the context of activities like play and sport which can never ensure safety from harm and where the use of the word "safe" will inevitably misinform someone.'[9] He goes on to explain that because people have so many different things in mind when we talk about safety, we have not yet agreed on a common definition. For example, 'safety' may be defined as the absence of accidents, by the achievement of targets or by compliance with standards and codes of practice. And in August 2006, the HSE went further and urged people to 'get a life' and to stop using health and safety as a blanket to prevent people doing worthwhile and enjoyable things.[10] The Commission announced a set of principles showing that it was not possible to create a totally risk-free society and people should not be scared of doing things by exaggerated trivial risks. The Commission emphasized that preventing accidents was more about recognizing real risks, then tackling them in a balanced way. The aim was to help keep people safe – not to stop the activities that were felt to be important. In promoting the message on their website, one example the HSE used was that of children playing conkers, saying that the risk of harm was incredibly low and 'not worth bothering about'.

For some people, 'safety' implies 'no accidents' – what Tim Gill called zero risk – whereas others would regard this position as potentially damaging to children. The Free Play Network[11] holds frequent discussions about the benefits of play and what gets in the way of good play experiences. Contributor Bernard Spiegal[12] has turned the safety argument on its head and says that given what we know about what children and young people need for play, it is surprising that 'no negligence claims have been lodged against local authorities for inducing boredom in children, or for limiting the scope of their imaginations, or for unreasonably denying them access to acceptable levels of risk in their play provision'.[13]

These views are perhaps best concluded by reference to research done by Rob Wheway in which he challenges some of the assumptions about children's playgrounds.[14] Wheway's research suggests that despite common perceptions, playgrounds are more exciting and adventurous compared with 20 years ago. He says that well-designed playgrounds, close to children's homes are still well used. Wheway comments that while parents want to 'keep an eye on children' to keep them safe, they also want exciting opportunities for children to play with. In other research,[15] children have also shown that they wanted more challenge and adventure in their play. Wheway's report indicates that most problems with children using the environment come down to unrealistic fears from parents based on lack of information and the all pervasive presence of the motor vehicle.

Traffic

One area where parents' perceptions match reality is that of the increase in vehicle traffic on the streets. Since the deregulation of buses and the privatization of the national rail system in the 1980s, the number of motor vehicles in use within the UK rose to over 30 million by 2002 (or one for every two people in the population). This use has had a significant impact on children's freedom to play and safety. Research by Rob Wheway and Alison Millward[16] has indicated that the decline in 'playing out' in the UK is mainly due to increased traffic and because motor vehicles are given priority over pedestrians, even in residential areas.

Roads are choked with cars making it difficult for children to play out on the street as was common 40 years ago, but the vehicles also contribute to child deaths. While the numbers are dropping, the latest figures suggest that around 120 child pedestrians are killed each year in the UK, with around 5,000 children being seriously injured. According to the Automobile Association,[17] in 1981 over 11,000 children were killed or seriously injured; by 2001 that had fallen to just over 5,000. The UK government has a target to reduce accidents to 3,000 by 2010, but mainly through a programme of child education rather than a reduction in the number of vehicles on the roads. If we listen to children, they want something different; they would prefer safer streets close to where they live, where they can be seen by family and relatives.[18]

Key questions

Look back to the questions that you answered at the start of this chapter. Think about your list with these questions in mind:

- How many items on your list need resources or equipment to be implemented?
- How many items are belief based or attitudinal; caused by how people think about play or children?
- What do you think should be done to help improve play for children?

Adult concerns of the kind described have adversely contaminated the environment for play and so affected children's capacity to play out. When children do play out, rather than ranging through an open, natural environment as Alan reports at the start of this section, many children are limited to 'play enclaves', smaller spaces set aside for children to play on designed playground equipment rather than in woods and streams. Children are not allowed to travel far from their homes for the reasons shown above, but also because of a change in the use of vehicle traffic. There is some good news, where traffic is slowed or cut off altogether, children return to the streets. And other countries have different solutions, as will be explained in Chapter 4 'Playing actively'.

Notes

1. This information was based on David Batty (2005) 'Timeline: a history of child protection' *The Guardian*, Wednesday 18 May 2005.

2. Rideout VJ, Vandewater EA and Wartella EA (2003) 'Zero to Six: Electronic Media in the Lives of Infants, Toddlers and Preschoolers' Kaiser Family Foundation Report. 28 October. Quoted in *The Biologist*, 54 (1), February 2007.

3. Quoted in *The Biologist*, 54 (1), February 2007.

4. At The Play England conference in the UK in 2006, Richard Lumb, Chairman of the Association for Play Industries reported that the API had prepared figures that showed that £165 million was spent each year in the UK on play spaces. Of that figure, £55 million was spent on equipment, £50 million on rubber surfaces and around £12 million on fencing.

5. The Health & Safety Executive Report 426, 2002 *Playgrounds – Risks, Benefits and Choices* (2002) Prof. David Ball found no convincing evidence of a change in playground accident statistics over the decade 1988–1998. He stated (Section 7.4.), *'[impact absorbing surface] products... would appear not to satisfy simple cost-benefit criteria'.*

6. According to the NSPCC, 7 per cent of children experience serious physical abuse at the hands of their parents or carers during childhood (Cawson P and others 2000) [Online] accessed 5 May 2007 from www.nspcc.org.uk

7. Tim Gill (2007) *No Fear: Growing Up in a Risk-Averse Society* London: Gulbenkian.

8. Play Safety Forum (2002) *Managing Risk in Play Provision: A Position Statement* London: Children's Play Council.

9. The Health & Safety Executive Report 426, (2002) as quoted above.

10. The full statement from the Health & Safety Executive dated 22 August 2006 is accessible from www.hse.gov.uk/press/2006/c06021.htm

11. The Free Play Network is a network of individuals and organizations, which aims to promote the need for better play opportunities for children. Accessed from www.freeplaynetwork.org.uk/index.html

12. Bernard Spiegel is principal of PLAYLINK and Common Knowledge. PLAYLINK is an independent play consultancy working in the areas of play space design, local engagement, policy, strategy, fundraising and general consultancy. See www.playlink.org.uk

13. In Green Places Magazine Article: 'The starting point for play' Available from www.playlink.org.uk/articles/?p=18

14. Rob Wheway (2007) *Urban Myths about Children's Playgrounds* London: Child Accident Prevention Trust.

15. John McKendrick (2000) 'The dangers of safe play Children 5–16' *Research Briefing No 22*, Economic and Social Research Council.

16. Rob Wheway and Alison Millward (1997) *Child's Play Facilitating Play on Housing Estates* London: Chartered Institute of Housing/Joseph Rowntree Foundation.

17. AA Motoring Trust, 2003 accessed 5 May 2007 from www.theaa.com/public_affairs/reports/facts_about_road_accidents_and_children.pdf

18. Cole-Hamilton I, Harrop A and Street C (2002a) *Making the Case for Play – Gathering the Evidence* London: National Children's Bureau pp. 70–72.

3 Why is play valuable?

Play can be fun or serious. Through play children explore social, material and imaginary worlds and their relationship with them, elaborating all the while a flexible range of responses to the challenges they encounter. By playing, children learn and develop as individuals and as members of the community.

Best Play *(2000)*[1]

Playing is what children (and other humans) do to find out about themselves and the world around them. We can guess that the play drive has something to do with human development and survival, but why children play certain games at specific times is not predictable, despite what is written about developmental 'ages and stages'. Children always *choose* to play; they cannot be made to play. The child needs to engage at some level with the playing activity or it is not play. As we have seen, sometimes the playful activity may start with another such as a friend or parent, but it only becomes play from the participant's point of view when *they* become playful, when they engage with the activity for their own reasons, and they decide when to stop playing.

Playing has a specific nature that sets it apart from directed tasks and – like a closely guarded recipe – the nature of play is a combination of many factors. Some of these factors are immediacy, concentration, choice, control, personal needs and completion; the exact combination of which will vary from each child and each activity.

The ingredients of playing

- Immediacy of action and response to that action is important. Play is about 'now' – children become immersed, engrossed in the play process to the exclusion of all other needs; their concentration becomes more focused.
- Choice is clearly a factor; free choice is best but often choice between alternatives is sometimes all that is needed.
- A sense of control is linked to choice; if children can control what they are doing they can choose how to change it or stop it.
- In choosing when to stop the activity children know when it has met their needs; the goal may not have been explicit at the start but they know when it is being reached (they may not get there). Accomplishment is self defined; it's not set by others. Taking on a new activity at which failure is certain, or being interrupted before they are finished soon leads to frustration. On the other hand, doing something that is too easy may also be irritating or unrewarding.
- Timelessness; time changes for playing children who will forget about its passing. How often do playing children say, 'I didn't realize what time it was' when they come home later than expected? They may also forget about eating, drinking or even going to the toilet.

The mix of factors changes because playing behaviour changes and the length of the playful activity may vary from a few seconds to many days. Play can be fun or it can be serious; fun if rules are being challenged or broken, serious if children are absorbed in a tricky activity. Play can be solitary or involve others; it can involve physical or mental activity. It may be creative or destructive; it may be about control of the individual or about control of others. It may also be about the absence of control or 'wildness' and chaos. These extremes are what make playing interesting – and especially what make working with playing children interesting. They are also what cause a lot of disagreement among people describing play. How can we begin to make sense of all this variety in play?

A moment of play

In a local sports centre, two 12-year-old boys were horsing around, slapping each other with towels. A young family walked past and the 5-year-old said, 'Dad, did you see the hairdryer?' Dad said, 'Yes...' then his son started singing to himself, 'Hair dry-er, hair dry-er-er.' When they had gone, the older boys picked up and repeated the hairdryer refrain, laughing softly to themselves.

Ways of looking at play

There are several explanations about the purpose of play, many of which see play as a process to help with development, whatever the expected result. Brian Sutton-Smith has identified over 300 forms of play and has categorized these into the leading opinions – what he calls rhetorics – and listed them as follows:[2]

- Play as Progress – growing and developing through play
- Play as Fate – chance or destiny (whether physical or metaphysical) controls all outcomes
- Play as Power – exploring status and conflict
- Play as Identity – looking at the identity and relationships of the players
- Play as the Imaginary – expressing flexibility and creativity
- Play as Exploration of the Self – for the pleasure and satisfaction of the player
- Play as Frivolous – the opposite of work, a challenge to work and all that it represents.

People interested in how humans function as animals, that is biologists, will point to the physiological and survival aspects of play, arguing that play is essential for the human child to grow into a fully developed human being. Psychologists, people interested in the workings of the mind, will highlight how playing helps the intellectual development of the child. Anthropologists will demonstrate that human cultural activities are strengthened and celebrated through play. Sociologists will talk about how play helps children with their status within relationships and networks. Our lived experience as humans is both simpler and more complex than that:

- our physical abilities impact on our thoughts;
- our thoughts affect our cultural development;
- our sense of belonging affects our power relationships with others;
- our relationships determine how we use and move through the world.

For example, in the small story from the sports centre above, we see two boys playing 'rough and tumble' which is both physical and social in nature. Physical as it involves carefully timed 'hits' with a towel that are playful without intending to harm, social as it is also about the boys playing with status – who's in charge, who's the leader. Independently another smaller boy then seeks his father's approval by drawing attention to the hairdryer and then plays creatively with the sound of the word 'hairdryer'. This interchange cues another game with the older boys where they mimic his song as a way of bonding with each other. And all this happens within a 30-second time frame.

Are all the experts right? Can playing do all these things? Well, yes it can because playing is a *process* not a product; playing is a way of doing things and not an end in itself. So it is possible to be playful when exploring identity, when using our bodies, when creating images and when interacting with each other and the world around us. It is also true that it is possible to do all those things without being playful. Quite often the playful mode is when children feel they are free to make their own choices without intervention from others. The difference can be obvious or subtle but is usually recognized by people who have spent some time with children or who remember what it was like to play themselves. As we have seen, play cues are a useful way to recognize that a child wants to play, but to recognize the activity as playful, we need to read the intent of the playing child and to believe that the child 'knows' what they are doing; we should see them as the experts in their own play.

Activity: Aspects of Play

- Think about an example of play that you have seen recently.
- Think about who was playing, who with and how they were playing.
- Make notes for yourself; you may find it useful to reflect on your example as you read on.

The Integral Play Framework

One model that draws together all these differing views on the purpose of play and gives them equal weight in the child's life is the Integral Play Framework. Building on the work of philosopher Ken Wilber,[3] this framework shows that the internal world of *feelings* for the child is as relevant as the world of *objects* shared with others. Wilber has produced a model that brought together the sciences with the arts; hard facts with personal opinions. It more accurately represents the whole human experience where, for example, we know that snow is frozen water (fact) but can often appear beautiful (opinion). Figure 3.1 shows the Integral Play Framework and balances the experiences of the child in the tangible world of structures with the insubstantial world of feelings and beliefs. As children are playing they are using their bodies to move through and experience the world, either solitary or with others. Those sensations are processed internally and inform the child's self-awareness, feelings and beliefs, which may be shared with others. For example; a group of children are playing chase, a physical game involving running around on the ground and over obstacles to evade capture. Ethan is 'it'; he is trying hard to pass the role to another and races round energetically. Initially frustrated that he cannot catch the others, he becomes elated when he tags his friend Sohail and manages to escape onto a high platform. Later he and Sohail talk about the game and what it felt like to be 'on' and what it was like when they were running away.

Like all humans, the playing child has an experience of the world that is both emotional and physical at the same time; we live at the boundary of the personal and shared worlds. And as has been commented by many writers, this integrated model recognizes that humans create their own world in relation

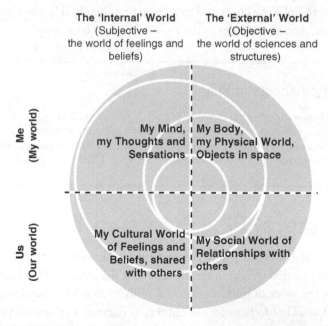

Figure 3.1 The Integral Play Framework

to that of other people; we are social animals who see our identity and status in relation to others. We should note that these are mutual worlds, different sides of a similar coin – <u>we shape and are shaped by our lived experience of mind, body and environment, as we integrate our different experiences of the world, they have an effect on who we are.</u> A useful metaphor might be a comparison with a seed; the small seed contains within it the potential to grow to full size and beauty as a flower. Yet without the right soil, water and light, that potential is limited or lost by factors surrounding the seed. While those factors are not part of the seed, they have significant impacts on its growth. Figure 3.1 shows the Integral Play Framework and how the various aspects of the child's world are interrelated.

For example, when a child is exploring textures in the world, say by painting a picture, they are using their body to move themselves and objects in the surroundings. There is sensory experience (feeling) and muscle control in both the bodily movement and the touch sensation of using paint and tools. These physical actions may simultaneously result in internal satisfaction for the child at either the resulting picture or the artistic pleasure it brings. And depending on circumstance, the child may expect others nearby to comment on the activity and resulting picture in a way that may be pleasing (or restricting) for the child. This is not to imply that every playful activity does all these things, but the example shows how complex and interrelated even simple activities may be; the feedback and satisfaction that children get from their playing may change moment to moment. Figure 3.2 shows this example set out in the Integral Play Framework.

Again please note that Figure 3.2 should not be read as the child consciously thinking or experiencing these things each time they carry out an action; the model shows how interrelated and embedded each of the actions is in the mind and body of the child and the surrounding environment – each has implications for and impacts on the other. Contrast this activity from two perspectives, one where the child does a painting for their own reasons and another where they do it as part of a cultural event (say Halloween or Diwali). In the first perspective, the primary 'worlds' involved would be the individual, the use of imagination and control of body. In the cultural event, they may be striving to draw an accurate representation of a cultural icon such as a pumpkin or lantern – the use of mind and body for artistic production are still there but they are now overlaid with the desire to produce a satisfactory image. And of course 'satisfactory' will be a combination of the child's feeling about the image and the audience's – children will often destroy art works that they do

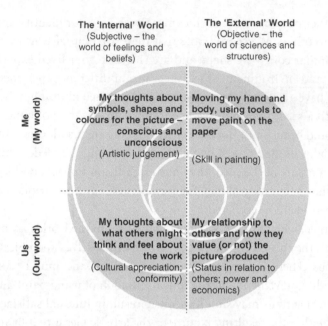

Figure 3.2 Painting a picture and the Integral Play Framework

not feel are suitable; and adults can destroy the satisfaction that children have taken from a carefully produced image by an unconscious critical remark.

We can now see why the different experts see differing things in play; each is looking at only part of the whole. Children will be playing with different experiences and parts of their world; it is when we observe the behaviour they exhibit that labels are put on that play to describe it as developmental, imaginary or frivolous. If we are to truly support the playing child, we should be open to what they want to play with and if we are facilitating environments, we should aim to give children a wide range of stimulating play opportunities that they may choose from – or not!

Key questions

Think about an example of play that you have seen:

- What was the physical activity involved in the play? What skills were used?
- Who was involved? Who was leading the play? If roles changed, how and when did they change?

- What emotion did you see on the faces of the players?
- How did they share ideas, if at all?
- Did the play involve one or more of these elements? If so, which were more dominant?

Levels of ability and understanding

The Framework also suggests that play functions at different 'levels' from very basic to quite complex according to our ability, understanding and confidence. While these levels are influenced by the age we are at, our age does not dictate what we are able to play with; this is not an 'ages and stages' model. While the model suggests that some abilities are generally developed before others, it recognizes that it is possible to have a moment when we exceed expectations in any part of our lives. This may be in our physical abilities, our thoughts, our sense of belonging or our power relationships with others – or all areas at the same time!

> In play a child always behaves beyond his average age, above his daily behaviour. In play it is as though he were a head taller than himself. (Lev Vygotsky 1933)[4]

Many of the actions in play may be repetitions of behaviour that we find pleasurable, interesting or within our current ability level, though at times we are able to make leaps to new levels of activity. When playing we may act above our ability; we toss a three-point ball into the basketball net that may take years of practice to replicate. We 'act out' pretending to be angry about going to bed in a manner that would be worthy of an actor at the National Theatre. Yet there is also a truth about the abilities that we usually display. A baby playing with food may produce patterns that are random expressions of the hand movements they made; we can guess that they do it to see what happens and because it feels good. An older child playing with paint or clay may similarly be making random patterns or may be creating a picture or scene based on reality or their imagination. While the older child can play randomly with patterns, the baby cannot play symbolically with pictures. Similarly a baby may only bond with immediate family members, while an older child may make friendships outside the extended family of home and community, and yet still feel part of the immediate family. As we get older we

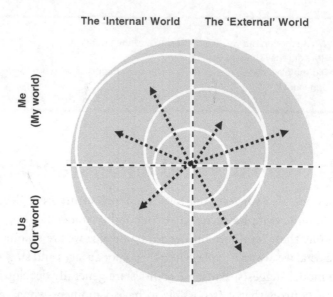

The 'Internal' World   The 'External' World

Me (My world)

Us (Our world)

Figure 3.3 Levels of ability and understanding

pick up more experiences that add to our 'portfolio' of skills and abilities that shape who we are and what we can do. It may be that we get 'stuck' because we are afraid or lack confidence to try new things, to take risks; we may have a 'comfort zone' where we operate mainly in one area or level; we may lack knowledge due to previous limited experience – or we may find our play cues restricted or dominated by others. All these barriers may affect our ability to play out the way we want to.

The areas we may reach in our play are suggested by the arrows and circles in Figure 3.3. The arrows are the peaks of ability that we can occasionally reach; the circles are the types of ability that we often display.

Using the Integral Play Framework, we can now start to look at the benefits we can see from the different forms of play – physical, psychological, social and cultural.

Why playing matters to our bodies

Children like to use their bodies in play, first to move around and then to move things; given half a chance, they are compelled to play with the natural elements in the environment. They love to move through the world feeling the earth beneath their feet, the rain, wind and sun on their faces. They love to play with the 'things' of the world: sticks, leaves, flowers, pebbles, mud,

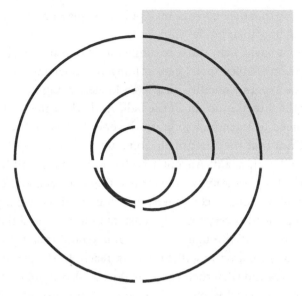

Figure 3.4 Playing actively

Figure 3.5 Exploring the world

water; anything that they move or manipulate. By playing like this they begin to understand how their bodies work.

Think about how a baby starts reaching for an object, say a ball on a table in front of them. Babies spend ages coming to understand that the object 'out there' is a separate identity, then even longer trying to get their arm to go in the right direction to touch the ball. And when the arm in the right place, they need to learn how to grasp the object. It is by 'playing' with all the possibilities that they eventually come up with the right combination, but then they lose it again! Anyone who has seen young children trying to get something they want knows how frustrating this trial and error process may be. Babies are not like computers; they don't find the 'right programme' and repeat it perfectly every time. By constant practice, the action eventually becomes 'natural' and through that, they understand that a similar process can be used to grasp anything that is within reach. In the process they learn about themselves and what their body can do, but also about things out in the world like gravity, velocity, angles, direction and dimension.

Our bodies react to this process and the more we play with them, the more we find we are able to do as we get older; muscles develop, tendons stretch and our bodily awareness is developed and extended especially through the senses. We learn to differentiate very subtly the sounds, smells and tastes that surround us. It's also true that not using our bodies in this way restricts the opportunities we have. If we don't use our bodies we don't find out what they can do; our strength is reduced and our sense of balance is diminished. Children in the middle years who have not played actively may find that they cannot keep up with others on the balance beam, in races or riding a bike. We'll look at this more in the chapter 'Playing actively'.

Why playing matters to our minds

As young humans start playing with their bodies, they simultaneously start to play with their minds. Very young babies act on instinct and in reaction to very simple perceptions; movement, light/dark, warmth/cold, food/hunger. But as soon as they start to move through the world, they begin to make sense of it; everything is a problem to be solved or a challenge to be overcome. Not only is this process necessary for us to begin to develop symbols for the world so that we can learn to hear words and then name things for ourselves, but research with animals has shown that this playful development actually shapes the way the brain works.[5] The more we play in our early years, the

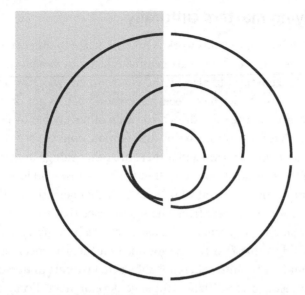

Figure 3.6 Playing through feelings and thoughts

bigger our brains become and the more connections we can make (sadly this capacity slows down around the time we are 5 years old).

With this capacity, we develop the full range of emotions of which humans are capable – from anger, fear, disgust, sadness and shame through to surprise, enjoyment and love. While these emotions are played out through our bodies and in relation to others, they are also formed in our minds and by our perceptions of what we see and feel. Our minds also make it possible for us to understand symbols so that we are able to communicate first in sounds, then spoken words and later in writing. It is not by accident that our species is called the 'wise human' – *homo sapiens*. Our minds make it possible for children to understand the difference (and make the connection) between the trunk with leaves that we see and touch as 'tree', the crude circles and lines that represent 'tree' in a drawing and the syllables 'tr-ee' that we use to describe the plant and 't-r-e-e' that we can write in letters. While we can be supported to do these things, it is only when they make sense to us that the whole picture falls into place. So playing helps the mind to develop and helps our comprehension of the world we inhabit. Many theorists have written about the importance of playing for intellectual, cognitive and emotional development. We'll look at this more in the chapter 'Playing through feelings and thoughts'.

Why playing matters culturally

Connected to how our minds work is how we relate to others culturally and creatively. The way we think is determined partly by the physical nature of our brains, by genetics but also by the environment we grow up in and the people around us. As we have seen, very young babies act or react to very simple perceptions; they are drawn towards other people to feed and care for them. At first they cannot see or differentiate objects very well, but quite quickly babies begin to realize that there are other things in their world and start to use their minds to work it all out. They know who looks after them, who cares most for them and who feeds (and changes!) them. They are able to identify family members from the sea of faces that surround them. The sounds and smells of parents and close relations become very familiar and bond the child to that family. The sounds that the baby hears and attempts to copy begin to form into coherent babbles that parents understand as communication prior to identifiable language development. Every child on the planet has the ability to speak any one of the thousands of languages and dialects that humans use. Children play with the noises they can make as they begin to communicate with others. It is as they begin to make sense of the rhythm and pattern that surrounds them that they learn the beginnings

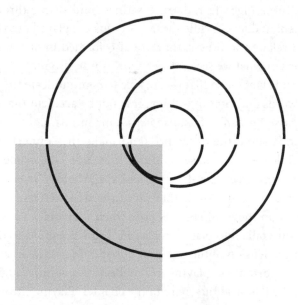

Figure 3.7 Playing through culture

of the relevant language, be it Chinese, Russian, Urdu or English.[6] At the same time, they are learning the cultural values of the family and community that use that language.

Children make sense of the world based on the relationships and models they find around them. Play begins as they find out about immediate family members, then their local community and finally people in the wider world. There are many debates about the influence of nurture on children and how much the way children are raised influences the way they think and behave, but many theorists accept that children learn the values of their community from the world they are in; as has been said – it takes a whole village to raise a child.[7] Children need to know the 'rules' of the village if they are to understand the community they grow up in. The same things may mean different things symbolically to different children, for example, the colour white has different meanings in different cultures.

Figure 3.8 Who am I?

English children know that white is the colour of the bride's dress in a traditional Christian wedding, yet for Indian children white is the colour used for funerals. It is these fundamental understandings that children use in their cultural play. They will play with the meanings of symbols, they will play with roles – boys can be police officers or girls; girls can be mummies or daddies. The creative abilities used in play will vary as will the kinds of play with imagination and fantasy – Red Riding Hood, *Star Wars* or the Tales of the Monkey King. We'll look at this more in the chapter 'Playing through culture'.

Why playing matters socially

When we play with others, we are soon aware of their relationship to us. Young children will happily play on their own, but as they become competent walkers and talkers they start to seek out others to play with. As they grow, children become conscious of the different relationships in the world; me and my mum, me and my family, my family and our friends. They find out who's in their 'gang' and who's not. Many games help children play with relationships to see how it feels to be 'king of the castle' and 'it' – the one

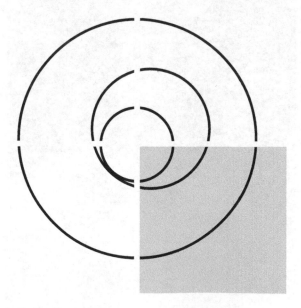

Figure 3.9 Playing with others

having to do all the chasing. There has been a lot of debate in recent years about competition between children, and rightly there has been a move to stop bullying and other forms of social abuse. There was also a move away from competitive games and 'zero tolerance' of playfighting was introduced, with 'rough and tumble' play being outlawed in some play settings. But it is now recognized that by and large boys and girls play differently when they socialize.[8]

While children will still express their individuality, on the whole girls prefer to play more quietly and in smaller groups, boys will run around and tend to make more noise. Group play with girls can still be competitive, but it tends to be expressed emotionally rather than physically; for example, arguing about who should be Mum or Dad in their games. Boys will engage in playfighting and rough and tumble play; not unlike young pups playing in a pack. Again research has shown that playfighting occasionally turns into real fighting, though that likelihood is much less than supervising adults predict. Children need to find out for themselves how the social order operates and play is a good process for working it all out.

Significantly there has also been a move in recent years by adults working with children to introduce them to the social structures they will use as they grow up; awareness has been growing of the child's right to comment on the world around them.[9] All over the UK, there are projects that help children's voices be heard. Circle time or children's councils[10] are active in many schools and children's service teams have participation officers whose role is to support children's consultation work and youth councils. We'll explore this more in the chapter 'Playing with others'.

Different types of play – *play types*

Having looked from different perspectives at why playing is valuable, we will now examine how children play in more detail. In order to help identify and describe different play behaviours, we will be referring to *Play Types*.

We've all seen groups of children running around in a game of tag, and we've seen individuals sitting alone concentrating on something in their hand; even though they are very different activities, we recognize both as forms of play. To help us see and describe the different sorts of play that children exhibit, Bob Hughes read through many books on human development and play to produce a list of play types.[11] He describes play types as the different behaviours that we see when children are playing.[12] Hughes originally identified 15 play types and then added recapitulative play in 2002 to make 16. The full list is as follows:

Communication play. Play using words, nuances or gestures. For example, mime, jokes, play acting, mickey taking, singing, debate, poetry.

Creative play. Play which allows a new response, the transformation of information, awareness of new connections, with an element of surprise. For example, enjoying creation with a range of materials and tools for its own sake.

Deep play. Play which allows the child to encounter risky or even potentially life-threatening experiences, to develop survival skills and conquer fear. For example, leaping onto an aerial runway, riding a bike on a parapet, balancing on a high beam.

Dramatic play. Play which dramatizes events in which the child is not a direct participator. For example, presentation of a TV show, an event on the street, a religious or festive event, even a funeral.

Exploratory play. Play to access factual information consisting of manipulative behaviours such as handling, throwing, banging or mouthing objects. For example, engaging with an object or area and, either by manipulation or movement, assessing its properties, possibilities and content, such as stacking bricks.

Fantasy play. Play, which rearranges the world in the child's way, a way which is unlikely to occur. For example, playing as being a pilot flying around the world or the owner of an expensive car.

Imaginative play. Play where the conventional rules, which govern the physical world, do not apply. For example, imagining you are, or pretending to be, a tree or ship, or patting a dog which isn't there.

Locomotor play. Movement in any and every direction for its own sake. For example, chase, tag, hide and seek, tree climbing.

Mastery play. Control of the physical and affective ingredients of the environments. For example, digging holes, changing the course of streams, constructing shelters, building fires.

Object play. Play which uses infinite and interesting sequences of hand–eye manipulations and movements. For example, examination and novel use of any object, that is, cloth, paintbrush, cup.

Recapitulative play. Play that is a recap of aspects of collective human evolutionary history. For example, rituals, fire making, den/cave making, using weapons, caring for other species.

Figure 3.10 Conquering fear

Role play. Play exploring ways of being, although not normally of an intense personal, social, domestic or interpersonal nature. For example, brushing with a broom, dialling with a telephone, driving a car.

Rough and tumble play. Close encounter play which is less to do with fighting and more to do with touching, tickling, gauging relative strength, discovering physical flexibility and the exhilaration of display. For example, playful fighting, wrestling and chasing where the children involved are obviously unhurt and giving every indication that they are enjoying themselves.

Social play. Play during which the rules and criteria for social engagement and interaction can be revealed, explored and amended. For example, any social or interactive situation which contains an expectation on all parties that they will abide by the rules or protocols, that is, games, conversations, making something together.

Socio-dramatic play. The enactment of real and potential experiences of an intense personal, social, domestic or interpersonal nature. For example, playing at house, going to the shops, being mothers and fathers, organizing a meal or even having a row.

Symbolic play. Using symbols in play to represent other 'real' objects. This play supports children's control, gradual exploration and increased understanding, without the risk of being out of their depth. Examples include using a piece of wood to symbolize a person, or a piece of string to symbolize a wedding ring.

It may seem that different forms of play may meet the criteria for eligibility as a specific play type; playing with fire can be seen as mastery, deep play or recapitulative play. Bob Hughes recognized this in his latest update on Play Types,[13] and described the original list as the 'basic or singular' play types (more will be said on this later). However using the descriptions in the taxonomy helps us identify the characteristics of different forms of play; children running around could be described as locomotor play but if we see interaction between the children and call it rough and tumble, it helps us identify a different dynamic in the play. The play types are included here as they give a clear description of the various forms of play that playing children may demonstrate and will be used in the following chapters, where we will look at playing actively, playing in our minds, being creative and playing with others.

Activity: Identifying play types

Observe a child or group of children playing, making notes of what they are doing.

- Could you identify from the children's behaviour which play types may have been present?
- How did you identity those play types, what evidence was there?
- Did the play change while you were watching? Did the play type change?
- How many different play types did you see?

Notes

1. This opening quote was taken from *Best Play* (2000) NPFA/CPC/Playlink, London UK. *Best Play* describes how children benefit from play opportunities and how play services and spaces can provide these benefits for children.
2. In his playfully written book, *The Ambiguity of Play* (1997) London: Harvard University Press Brian Sutton-Smith explored the various 'rhetorics' of play. The book makes the case that while

we may not know the root cause of play, adults describe the resulting play behaviours in several key ways, the rhetorics of play:

> The word *rhetoric* is used here in its modern sense, as being a persuasive discourse, or an implicit narrative, wittingly or unwittingly adopted by members of a particular affiliation to persuade others of the variety and worthwhileness of their beliefs. (Sutton-Smith 1997 p. 8)

3. For more information, see Ken Wilber (2000) *Integral Psychology* Boston: Shambhala. In brief, Wilber has studied both Eastern and Western philosophies and sciences and has produced a model that shows the complementary and integrative qualities of these approaches.

4. Lev Vygotsky (1933) *Play and Its role in the Mental Development of the Child* p. 12.

5. Commenting on work with rats, Gopnik and colleagues state that: 'The new scientific research...does suggest, though, that a radically deprived environment could cause damage...a brain can physically expand and contract and change depending on experience.' This was taken from Alison Gopnik, Andrew N Meltzoff and Patricia Kuhl (1999) *How Babies Think: The Science of Childhood* London: Weidenfield and Nicholson p. 182. This work has now been supported by brain scanning techniques used on humans.

6. For more on language development, look at *How Babies Think: The Science of Childhood* as quoted above Chapter 4.

7. The 'It takes a village...' proverb was used by Hillary Rodham Clinton in 1996 as the title of a book about valuing children's unique contributions to society. The sentiment is also key to the *More is Caught Than Taught* (MCTT) approach for the care and development of young children developed by A. Jack Guilebeaux and delivered in the UK by the Inspire agency.

8. See, for example, Jennie Lindon (2001) *Understanding Children's Play* Cheltenham: Nelson Thornes Ltd.

9. The right for children to express their opinions on all matters that affect them is upheld by Article 12 of The United Nations Convention on the Rights of the Child, 1989.

10. Circle time is a group activity in which children sit in a circle with the purpose of sharing information about themselves and each other respectfully and fairly. Children's councils vary in style but aim to replicate the adult democratic process. Both methods are intended to give children a chance to discuss matters that affect them.

11. The list of 16 play types and explanations are adapted from those given in Bob Hughes (1996a) *A Playworker's Taxonomy of Play Types* (as quoted in *Best Play*, 2000) and added to in the Second Edition (2002) published by Play Education.

12. Bob Hughes (2006) *Play Types – Speculations and Possibilities* London: London Centre for Playwork Education and Training pp. 24–25. This is an update and extension of Bob's previous books on play types.

13. Bob Hughes (2006) as quoted above pp. 89–90.

4 Playing actively

Children need to be active and for most children it's easiest to be active outdoors. Children love to play outside. Given the chance, they are drawn to the environments of parks, woodlands, river banks and beaches as if by magic. There they can explore the elements – usually earth, air and water, with the occasional bit of fire – make and destroy empires, sit and watch the clouds go by, run and jump, roll and balance, test the current or climb a tree, whisper, talk, shout or scream – and every day is different. However for many children being active is fitted in around the constraints of modern living. While using our bodies is necessary for many forms of play, there are specific play types that support physical play; object play, exploratory play, locomotor play, rough and tumble, mastery and sexual play. Like all play types, these play behaviours complement and support each other. And while our ability to carry out these forms of play will be ultimately influenced by our body and so our physical capabilities, it is helpful to remember that how we (and others) think about the activity.

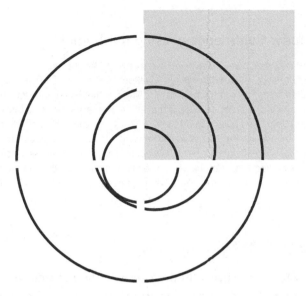

Figure 4.1 Playing actively

Figure 4.2 Playing actively

> ## Case study: Confidence in using our bodies
>
> Ali was recalling her own play experiences in the 1950s and how she felt she was not allowed to take physical risks as a child: 'Both my sister and I were taught to be afraid – "Be careful, be careful, be careful".' She felt that experience left her with a resistance to be active: 'I don't like heights at all; I'm not very surefooted because I lose confidence…and I very quickly say "I can't do that".'[1] Ali knew that she was physically capable of being active but that as a child she had not been encouraged to be active and she felt that had affected how she now approached extreme physical activity. Ali's personal story reflects some of the barriers to play that we looked at in Chapter 2. It is important that children are given the space and freedom to play from an early age.

Starting early

Being active early in life helps children develop their muscle mass and physical coordination. Children have a natural urge to move and be active as toddlers – athletes who try to keep up with children soon get worn out by the endless energy that toddlers seem to have.

Babies need to see things moving around them; from a few weeks after birth, mobiles suspended above a baby's cot will entertain them for hours as they look for the patterns and shapes created by the moving objects. But the movement needs to be random, if the mobile needlessly circulates with no variation, the baby will soon lose interest in it. And of course babies soon learn to recognize the faces of parents and familiar carers; the movement and variety of faces create endless fascination for babies in their early months. Babies learn to communicate with parents by mimicking facial expressions including smiles, eye widening and sticking out their tongue. As all parents know, babies can be entertained with simple games of peek-a-boo, where the parents can 'hide' behind their hands or a convenient cushion – the sudden movement and surprise is enough stimulation for young babies.

> ## Example: Treasure baskets for young children
>
> When children are very young, 'treasure baskets' can be very useful for supporting extended play frames through spontaneous and varied play. The treasure basket is usually a wicker or other handmade container, shallow enough for young children to reach into but large enough to contain a varied assortment of objects.
>
>

According to Eleanor Goldschmied,[2] the chief promoter of treasure baskets, the ideal sorts of objects are chosen for children to explore various sizes, shapes, textures, sounds, colours, smells and tastes. The objects should be 'real' rather than painted or plastic so that the child can explore the nature of the object. The 'treasure' may be made from both natural and manufactured materials. Examples include things from around the house like various wooden and metal spoons, spatulas, egg cups, bowls, pegs, napkin rings, a tea strainer, garlic squeezer, bunch of keys, whisks and weights; and natural things like large pebbles, pine cones, big shells, walnuts, an apple, orange, lemon, a small natural sponge, balls of wool and string. The basket will be more interesting if some of the objects are changed from time to time. The concept behind basket play is similar to Nicholson's 'theory of loose parts' – things that we can manipulate or move around (this is described more fully in 'Enhancing spaces for play' section).

Using our touch

When babies learn to grasp objects, they will begin to move the objects around, dropping them, banging them, exploring their textures, 'tasting' them and looking at the contrasting colours. This is an example of object play in which the child uses an endless and interesting sequence of coordinated hand-eye movements to find out the qualities of the object. Object play will continue for some time as the child finds out about the environment, about them and how objects act differently depending on their shapes, texture and mass. For example, children playing with sand learn that a little water helps make the sand more firm and so able to hold a shape necessary to build a castle or mould a shape; but too much water makes the sand 'sloppy' and too wet to make castles with. Using our hands in play helps us develop the fine skills needed to grasp and manipulate delicate objects; while an egg is not too heavy an object for children to carry, it can easily break if grasped with too much pressure. Playing with a variety of heavy and delicate objects builds a sensitivity in our bodies so that we 'know' how much strength to apply to pick up a delicate object but not so much that we crush it.

Moving around

Toddlers need to discover the world around them – being able to touch, explore and move through the world is critical to a toddler's healthy development; a restricted and inactive life is not best for children. Desmond Morris describes it like this; 'to be really successful as an adult, [the child] must be super-active in childhood, and it is...natural playfulness that encourages this'.[3]

One of the play types Bob Hughes has identified is *locomotor play* – physical movement in any and every direction for the fun and thrill of movement. Toddlers show this as they begin to move around – movement of itself is playful and exciting as they begin to take control of the bodies and thereby the environment they move through. As they grow, this form of play will include chasing games, the many forms of 'tag' or 'it', 'kick the can', hide and seek, rolling down hills, walking along the tops of walls and tree climbing.

Case study: Confidence in exploring the world

As young child, Andy often found himself playing in the family garden. His favourite play activity was climbing the apple tree that was there. The tree afforded him the chance to test his strength and confidence by getting higher and seeing what was happening over the fence. In Andy's case, this became a lifelong playful activity as he took up rock climbing as he became an adult.

When he grew older, Andy started playing in the street outside the house, ranging up to 300 metres away where the main road ran. He remembered playing in the alleyways between roads, then at age 7 walking to school with others in the street. Later still he learned to ride his bike to the local park.

Exploratory play

As children get older, object play will take in exploratory play, which is when children find out how things fit together and how different shapes and textures work with each other. Often this play will start off as taking things apart – it's a good way to help work out what goes where. In smaller children, this may be supported by making things with plastic bricks or other connecting shapes. This will continue for many years as the child gets to know their environment and the endless possibilities of the materials in it. It may develop into more complex play such as model making, knitting or den building. Playing with objects and exploring the environment, both need the child to be reasonably active to manipulate the objects as desired and to move around to collect the things necessary to build them together.

Rough and tumble play

An often misunderstood form of play is rough and tumble. It is included in this section on physical play for though it is also a form of social play in that it takes place between two or more players, rough and tumble is about and requires a fine degree of physical control to be carried out properly. The difference between a play wrestle and a real bear-hug is a degree of pressure that takes a level of subtlety to achieve. To give it another name, playfighting is carried out by many social animals; it is a way of practising fighting in a harmless fashion and helps the animal develop the skills necessary for defending themselves, mating and for hunting.

Playfighting is also common among other species; cats, dogs and monkeys to name a few. The characteristics of it are special signals that indicate 'this is playing' – a common indicator for playfighting across many species is that it is much exaggerated; there will be many wild and overstated movements – think of kittens and puppies leaping into the air when they play pounce – in the real thing animals are more still, focused on what is happening and saving their energy for the bout. And like humans, chimpanzees and dogs will indicate playfighting with open mouth signals. For example, when dogs are playfighting, they typically 'grin' with their lips pulled back in an exaggerated manner; what some writers call the 'play face'. In humans this signal has developed into smiling. These two features are common to the playfights of many animals including humans.

If we want to tell if a child's fight is real or not, we should look at the player's face – are they smiling or laughing; the face tells us if the battle is fun or serious. The second clue to the purpose of the activity is the stance taken by the players; are they 'bouncing around' or using exaggerated movements? Again in playfights these are very obvious; in the real thing there is a grim determination present which shows that one side or the other wants to win and is setting out to do so.

When the fight is over, in both animals and humans, the close physical contact initiated in the playfight often ends in 'grooming' activity, either real or ritualistic. In animals this may be nuzzling, licking or stroking; in humans, particularly small ones, those behaviours may also be apparent, as will face-to-face intimate conversations, collapsing in a heap, or exaggerated hugs and cuddles.

Other elements of rough and tumble, mainly but not exclusively carried out by boys, are touching, tickling, assessing relative strength, discovering physical flexibility and the exhilaration of display – acting out your emotions. Girls engage in different but no less intimate forms of physical contact, which are often based on close contact and personal communication and may include applying make-up and other trusting actions.

Rough and tumble play has been banned in some settings and is outlawed in some schools with a 'zero tolerance' policy where it is seen as too violent and 'unsafe'. Research has shown that 'play fighting' occasionally turns into real fighting, though much less than adults expect. Penny Holland[4] has written that adults often mistake playfighting for real fighting and step in to break up the 'incident', thus denying the children, often boys, their chance to play out the rough and tumble. And Steve Biddolph quotes work that shows that the male hormone testosterone may be a factor in why boys are more interested in physical competition and their rank among their peers.[5] Again while the issue needs further examination, it seems clear that children are driven by their nature to find out for themselves how their bodies work in relation to one another and play is a good process for working it all out.

Mastery play

This form of play encompasses two elements of the term mastery; the first is control over the physical actions necessary for the play and the second is the ability to change the environment around the player. Abilities will change with age, but even the simple act of making a sandcastle requires considerable physical control and dexterity – to dig the right amount of sand, place it accurately in the bucket, pat down the sand to compact it, then successfully turn over the lot so that not too much sand is lost, then to carefully remove the bucket. Increasing levels of physical strength and dexterity will be needed as mastery play also involves engagement with the four elements – earth, air, fire and water – so digging holes, constructing shelters, building fires and damming streams. Many of these activities require physical strength and/or speed and dexterity combined with determination to complete the task to 'overcome' the elements if they do not 'play' the way expected. Mastery play as well as being enjoyable for itself will also equip the player to change and adapt the environment the way the child desires; thus is it is also a form of recapitulative play, as digging, making fires and water courses are all survival skills that humans have needed for thousands of years. If we recognize this, we begin to see the importance of encouraging children to play outside and to explore the elements.

Sexual play

Another form of play that is not listed in the play types but is nevertheless very apparent to anyone who has seen children playing between 5 and 15 is sexual play. It is where children and young people, responding to the feelings and changes in their bodies and the expectations of their culture, play with roles and relations that may be with different sexes or the same sex. This is an aspect of play that is very rarely spoken of in practice as it can be a 'taboo subject' and is often annihilated (stopped) or adulterated (changed) by the adults present in the play frame. These adults may feel embarrassed or threatened by the possibility for sexual play by children who are exploring their bodies and their gender. This is not to say that adults should set up impromptu sex education classes, but more that they should not feel the need to immediately intervene in this aspect of play if it arises between children. What is playing in the home corner or 'mummies and daddies' if not the exploration of both social and emotional relationships? A natural extension of this may be the innocent kiss that one 'mummy' gave to 'daddy' during their play. This will be taken further by children as they move into puberty and realize that not all children are the same and they are more attracted to one type of person than another. Many young people of this age have learned as much about sex from the playground and party games like 'Kiss Chase', 'Spin the bottle' and teenage versions of 'Truth or Dare' as from the classroom or their parents. The play frame creates a safer environment in which to explore sexuality and the difference between girls and boys; any misunderstandings can be laughed away as being playful, so not serious. It speaks volumes about attitudes to children and sexual relations in the UK that so little has been written about this form of play. Perhaps society's insistence on seeing children as 'little adults' prevents us recognizing that children's relationships for them are real and their actions are happening now, in the present. Perhaps more openness in this area would help girls who are playing with conventional roles of femininity as 'virgin' or 'tart' and boys whose sexual fumblings can be at the extremes seen as embarrassing or overly aggressive.

Key questions

If you work with or have children of your own, these questions will need answering at some time or another – be prepared!

⇨

> ### Key questions—cont'd
>
> - What is your attitude to children playing with sexual roles and relations? Do you feel threatened by or curious about their actions?
> - Would you be challenged by overtly sexual behaviour between different children?
> - Would you need to comment on boys – or girls – wearing tutus or make-up? Would it depend on age or circumstance? If so, why?
> - Would you know how to talk to them about their behaviour? Would you know how to answer their questions about relationships with others?

Using our bodies actively

Playing actively is vital for the healthy development of our bodies and for the full utilization of our physical abilities. The need to develop delicacy and accuracy in our movements has been discussed above, yet we also need to use our large muscles as well. In earlier times, an ability to use our bodies to run, climb or fight may have made a difference between getting away or getting caught by predators. While children in the industrialized world may not face that kind of basic threat everyday, they are still at risk if they do not use their bodies actively. There has been much discussion about the 'obesity epidemic' facing British children in the twenty-first century and it is clear that there has been a change in activity levels between 1970 and 2000. Children on average became 70 per cent less active in that 30-year period.

In 2003 the UK's Chief Medical Officer, Sir Liam Donaldson stated that children needed to be active for at least 1 hour every day and it was reported that less than half of children were meeting the recommended minimum levels of activity.[6] Following up on this in 2005, the government white paper *Choosing Health* focused on reduced outdoor play opportunities as one of the contributory factors to childhood obesity. In 2004, Professor Roger Mackett showed through research with children aged 11–13 years that 'walking and playing provide children with more physical activity than most other activities'.[7] His report makes a strong argument for children to be physically active outdoors and for children to be supported to walk more to school and other activities. Mackett's research shows that walking to and from school can be better for children than 2 hours a week of structured games lessons. He also challenges the trend towards reduced (or no) school breaks by showing that they contribute to the overall amount of children's physical activity. And perhaps not surprisingly, research by Jane Wardle and colleagues (2006) has shown that children who become obese before the age of 11 tend to stay obese throughout their life.[8]

An important factor in how active children play is how they are treated by the key people in their lives. Research[9] indicates that if given access to physical play, young children believe that they can do most physical tasks if they try hard enough. This belief begins to change from the age of 8 years as children realize that no matter how hard they try, some people will be better (and some worse) than them – physical limits are beginning to have an effect. If children are self-motivated to play actively, that is, for the fun of it, they are likely to continue. However if they are graded into 'ability' by unsympathetic adults or peers – the typical story of being left until last when being chosen for the team – the evidence is that for a majority of children, they will stop or reduce their activity levels by the teenage years. And as the story of Ali shows, adult fears about safety have an impact on how active children may be. These attitudes have an impact on overall activity levels such that 70 per cent of children give up all physical activity or sport on leaving school. If we recognize the benefits of physical play in the environment for children, we should find ways to support that play so that children do not lose out.

Supporting access to the wider environment

It's simple: if we give children access to the environment they will play; and the better the quality of that environment, the better the opportunities for play. Fortunately, Bob Hughes has listed[10] the features of a high-quality environment for play, which include a wide variety of features and opportunities.

Example: The features of a rich play environment

- Access to the natural elements: earth, air, fire and water
- Choice of manufactured and natural materials: things to move around and things to use (paint, clay, paper, etc.)

Example—cont'd

- Opportunities for risk and challenge: in the physical environment, and in the social context between people and by yourself
- Chances for movement: running, jumping, balancing
- Places to express emotions: sadness and happiness, rejection and acceptance
- Stimulation for the senses: different sounds, smells and textures
- Playing with identity: dressing up, wearing masks whether real or pretend
- Chances for social interactions: opportunities for enhancing self-esteem and understanding
- Newness and change: building and demolishing, negotiating, cooperating
- Overall an interesting and varied physical and human environment
- 'Sufficient' space to do what is wanted. (Amended based on Bob Hughes 1996b)

Environments do not need to have all these features to be valuable for play, but the more features there are, the more varieties of play will take place. By letting children play, you will quickly come to see what is important for them. Treasure baskets (described above) provide a miniature version of a rich play environment that is stimulating for very young children. As children grow up they are drawn to a similar level of stimulation in the wider environment; touching, exploring and moving whatever is around. Children don't need technological toys if they have access to a good environment especially one that is natural and has plant or animal life. Recapitulative play – fire making, den building, using tools, interest in other animals – goes some way to explaining the attraction of the wider environment. Edward Wilson describes this fascination with natural things as 'biophilia', a focus on life and lifelike processes, a love of nature. This tendency helps make clear why spaces like woods and beaches are such good play environments.

> Most children have a bug period, and I never grew out of mine. (Edward O Wilson 1986)[11]

Where there is enough space for children to move around and enough materials for them to explore, all we need do is let the children play; themes and ideas will emerge naturally from their interests and from what they discover. We may need to supply tools if wanted such as spades and buckets (though often enough, hands will do), and may join in, if invited, for the play should always be led by the children. Depending on the age of the children, the extras we provide may be as

Figure 4.3 Swinging on a tree

simple as a bat and ball, a blanket or towel and food and a drink. Children who are lucky enough to live near land where they can play freely will soon develop a sense of what is needed for play. Walking through a small wood on the edge of a housing estate it is easy to spot the signs of playful activity; the tracks of bikes, the ropes in trees, dams in streams, patterns in mud or made from stones, the den or tree house and once in a while the scorch marks of a bonfire.

Two young children aged four and six were walking through the woodland with their father and a friend, also aged six. On seeing a fallen tree, the children ran off to explore, the older children quickly climbing the stouter lower branches. The younger child, a boy, saw what they were doing and followed on and soon all three children were decorating the branches, swinging on the limbs to make a see-saw movement. On the far side of the tree some other children had made a makeshift den by leaning broken branches against the trunk. The children eventually found this and began to explore, wondering who lived in such a palace. 'Fairies,' said one of them, and the play theme moved into a story about what the fairies did and how they lived. The friend told a 'true story' of how a fairy had died and her grandfather had left it on the back step of their house, and it was gone in the morning. The other two children listened fascinated and without cynicism, for they too wanted to see the fairies.

But of course not many children have free access to such places, being more used to roads, tarmac, playgrounds and parks. So how can we provide more playful opportunities in these places?

Using the environment

As we saw in Chapter 2, often the greatest barrier to children's playing is adult attitudes, whether from parents or other adults in the district. By simply saying 'yes' to play we make things happen, however if the adults choose to they can do so much more for children and their play.

In 2004 the Children's Play Council was promoting the *51 Minute Challenge* to show that children spend the largest proportion of their waking hours outside of school (which was calculated to take up 9 minutes of every waking hour between the ages of 0 and 16 years). It was in those 51 minutes that children are at home, in the after school club, the street or the playground and would often be playing. The challenge was intended to highlight to those in charge of the wider environment and play spaces the need for quality spaces to support children's play.

Supporting play means supporting the opportunities for play and so we need to help children use the environment that surrounds them, wherever that is. The easiest way to do this is to use the environment ourselves, ideally by using it on foot. Walking helps everyone keep active and also helps us see things better. Walking (or riding in a buggy) children find out who we talk to, where we go and how we conduct ourselves when outside. They note that when the weather gets bad we put on extra protection and that when the sun shines we take different precautions. They note who we speak to and who we don't; they become savvy in assessing the people who are out and about in the neighbourhood. Children learn how to cross the road by seeing what we do and how we behave, by showing them how to watch out for traffic and how to cross the road safely, we give them a life skill and help them become more independent.

Case study: A person friendly environment

In the Netherlands (as in some other parts of Europe), priority is given to pedestrians and cyclists. Motorized vehicle drivers must give way to cycles and pedestrians in many inner-city traffic environments. In a road accident between a bike and a car, the car driver is considered responsible; not unreasonable when we realize that a car can harm a pedestrian or cyclist much more than they can hurt the car. This attitude creates a positive approach to walking and cycling that contributes to over 85 per cent of the population in Amsterdam having a cycle.

But not only does the law help with walking and cycling; the road layout also helps greatly. On many town roads, cycle paths are built alongside the roadway for other traffic. They have their own traffic lights and crossings for major roads. Cars cannot park in the cycleway (as they often do in the UK). As a result, it is quite common to see children riding round town with parents, friends or by themselves. Parents will often carry one or two children with them on the bike, and very few people wear a 'safety' helmet, such is their confidence in the system. This ability to travel round independently gives children a great freedom that significantly enhances their play opportunities.

Sustrans the UK's leading sustainable transport charity works towards more sustainable transport across the country. The charity shows that as quarter of all journeys made by car are less than 2 miles long, 'converting' to walking or cycling would have great benefits for us and for the environment. Sustrans aims to promote cycling and walking as healthy forms of transport and is actively creating the National Cycle Network. In Bristol, the home of Sustrans and therefore benefiting longest from its work, almost 5 per cent of journeys to work are made by bicycle compared to the national average of 2.8 per cent. The growing support for this form of transport was shown in December 2007 when Sustrans won the public vote for the People's £50 Million Lottery Giveaway prize to develop the network further.

Most children will know (or can find out) the places to play close to home; by helping them understand the dangers of traffic we help keep them safer and extend considerably their range of play opportunities. These spaces for play might be the pavement outside the house, the spare land at the end of the street, a friend's garden or a local park or playground. These places can be used for a variety of playful activities that children have played for hundreds of years – exploring, chasing, hiding, constructing and socializing. Even if parents are busy working in the week, helping children to use the environment at weekends is time well spent for both adult and child; the adult can relearn how to be playful and the child's confidence can be extended with the support of the parent. Active habits can start early with visiting local friends, walking in the countryside or local parks and going cycling or swimming as a family. Later when children grow older and become independent they need to know how to make their own plans. Planning who to go with, what is needed and when to come back, all help children develop responsibility and make choices for themselves. They also need to know what to do if they are running late and parents can show them what to do, as can adults working with children. Many children carry mobile phones, but they need to know where to find help and who from if the battery goes down or if they run out of credit. Taking these sensible precautions helps children use the environment and stay safer.

Enhancing spaces for play

There will still be many children for whom the playground or the play park will be the only practical place to play and for many children their play will be in the presence of parents or other adults responsible for their care. For most children, the typical play space will be the home garden or the school playground. To add to these spaces, the easiest way is to bring in 'loose parts', materials and equipment to enhance or support the children's play. Simon Nicholson first described loose parts – the things that we can move around or change – and said that the 'more flexible an environment, the greater the level of creativity and inventiveness that it supports'.[12]

Of course just adding a grassed or 'natural' area to a tarmac playground will add considerably to its playfulness. The natural area will support other forms of life in vegetation or in small animals, it will show signs of growth and decay and it will change with the seasons – all these things can support forms of play. Even where gardens cannot be created natural features can be brought in with the use of plant buckets or troughs. No matter how small, these areas will provide stimulation for the senses by offering different sounds, smells and textures for children to experience. And some schools and nurseries even supply Wellington boots and rain macs so that outdoor play can continue all year round.

Learning through Landscapes is a national UK charity that helps schools make the most of their outdoor spaces for play and learning.[13] Their campaign has added significantly to the provision and use of the outdoor environment in schools in the UK. The adults working with Learning through Landscapes recognize that access to the natural elements is vital for children's play and learning.

With or without a natural space, children can create their own play from very basic materials such as sheets, rope and large wooden blocks. These may be bought as play materials or recycled from other uses. These large-scale 'loose parts' support changes in the environment such as den building. The materials may be used to build up new spaces for play and then 'demolished' to allow them to be remade every day. These activities are often carried out by children working together so often involve negotiation and cooperation.

Ideally the environment and loose parts would support any of the forms of children's play: active, social, creative or imaginative. Adding height with pallets, wooden boxes or climbing frames helps children explore the physical environment and gives opportunities for running, jumping and balancing. Climbing frames may be fixed but if they are moveable the children can use them in different ways for different forms of play. Many schools use wooden picnic tables as they are stable enough to climb on and may be used for a variety of purposes. These may be supplemented with balance beams and storytelling circles as space allows.

Case study: Changing environments

The creative partnership Snug and Outdoor, design dynamic and imaginative playgrounds and have been working with 'boring' school playgrounds for several years.[14] In the Experimental Playground (which was in Daubeney School, Hackney, London) Snug and Outdoor worked with children in the school using found material such as traffic cones, wooden pallets, chalk, fabrics and lights to transform the typical tarmac space into something special. This approach was used to make the changes permanent in 2004 with den-building areas, storytelling and performing areas, active areas and social areas. In a new development in 2007, Snug and Outdoor collaborated with playground equipment manufacturer Sutcliffe Play to create the SNUG kit, made up of nine large-scale, colourful and versatile sculptural shapes, which children can rearrange themselves. The SNUG kit (basically a collection of large 'loose parts') can be used separately, fitted together or used in combinations with each other. The product looked set to be a useful addition to the traditional tarmac playground where other more natural solutions were not allowed.

Not all changes require new equipment and new resources, for example, supplying children with a box of chalk is often enough to help them extend their play in active and creative ways. Chalk is a useful addition to a games box either kept at home or that a school may supply for playtime. Chalk may be used to write messages, tell stories, draw hopscotch patterns, snakes and ladders, noughts and crosses – and it all washes away in the rain so children can start again another day. Other useful items in a play box would be a variety of bats and balls, scarves or blankets, bean bags, rubber hoops, large dice – with these children can find a variety of ways to be playfully active outdoors.

Some changes may be more permanent. Children at a Sheffield school drew up a questionnaire to seek pupils' comments on developing the school playground. They negotiated photocopying through the headteacher and school clerk and every pupil was issued the questionnaire. After presentation of the ideas to the staff team and governing body, a series of changes were made. The results from the survey showed that the children had clear ideas about what they wanted for the tarmac playground. These included separation of the playground into different areas for active and social activities. One of the ideas was for playground markings using aerosol paint; floor markings helped with showing where football (especially) could be played. The tarmac was covered with yard games like snakes and ladders, number and alphabet trails and hopscotch. Simple platforms and seats were added to the playground to vary the height levels and provide places for the children to sit if they wished. Planting was slowly introduced through tubs and a nature garden to create quieter areas. The children spontaneously recognized that in addition to just running about, play can be useful to express emotions like sadness and happiness, and to face and deal with rejection and acceptance. The scheme was successful and the children's play opportunities were enhanced and conflicts lessened.

The play park

Outside of home and the school playground, children are expected to be found playing in the play provision provided for them by local authorities in parks or local playgrounds. These playgrounds while designed as playful spaces usually offer only limited opportunities for large-scale physical play on equipment such as swings, slides and climbing frames. Unless built in a site that has natural features, the flexibility of such spaces is often limited. While they would benefit from many of the features we have discussed for home and school playgrounds, public playgrounds are built to be much more robust, often cemented into the ground and with limited opportunities for change or transformation. In such spaces adults can support active play by carefully suggesting playful games and activities to encourage children to stay longer on the play equipment; though remember the children will only play what they want to play. Children may be taken to the playground on their own or with younger siblings. The more children present, the more the opportunity for child led interaction and activities, so check with neighbours to see if their children want to join you in the park. Children in groups will more easily set up teams that involve racing around the playground, taking it in turns on various pieces of equipment or seeing who can collect the most 'helicopters' from horse chestnut trees.

While being limited in the formal supply of loose parts available, playgrounds in public parks offer children the opportunity to engage with the elements, if not fire then certainly those of water, earth and air.

The large play areas often have a stream or water fountain nearby and it's quite easy for children to make rafts from leaves and twigs or to play 'pooh sticks' by racing twigs down the stream. Throughout the year it can be quite difficult to keep children away from water; they are drawn to it and in summer will wish to paddle or bathe in it whenever they see it. Many local authorities in the UK recognize this and provide water features in large public parks, including large paddling pools, fountains and purpose designed play equipment for the channelling and collection of water. In these places all that is needed is for the children to be given access to the feature. Some parents may find this easier to do if the children are dressed in washable clothes that are not too precious and allow the play to go where the children want it to. We should try to supervise the children without being controlling about how they want to play. As with all play, the more children experience elements in the environment, the more respect they will gain for those elements. The adults supervising young children at play should reassure themselves that there are no obvious hazards in or near the water though we should be aware of being so cautious that we remove the playfulness of the element. Adults who are working in a care role with children may need to carry out a risk assessment to ensure that all necessary actions have been taken to help make the feature safer for children.

Example: Risk assessment

A risk assessment is a check of the elements of an activity that could cause harm to people. All activities carry an element of risk. The aim of an assessment should be to judge whether the risk is reasonable when measured against the benefits of the activity and after any suitable precautions have been taken. The main elements of a risk assessment are as follows:

- Recognizing the people at risk, who may be those taking part or bystanders
- The hazard or hazardous activity, for example, a trailing cable or climbing a tree

---

Example—cont'd

- The potential risk – which should be real rather than trivial, for example, risk of harm or injury rather than the risk of a cut from a sheet of paper
- An assessment of whether the risk is a high, medium or low risk, for example, very likely to happen or quite rare
- An assessment of any control measures that will reduce the hazard, for example, securing the cable or assessing the strength of the tree
- The action to be taken to implement those control measures, that is, making sure it has been done
- A named person who is responsible for the work identified and the date it will be completed.

Using the elements

Playing with the earth in public can be a little harder than playing with water; park owners do not take kindly to children digging up their flower beds. However some authorities do encourage the use of sand near play equipment as a 'safety surface' and as a natural modelling material. Whatever its designed function, children will always use it in their play for its modelling and textural abilities. In one public park miles away from the sea in Oxford, a natural sand bank with a small stream has been used by generations of children for making dams and sandcastles. Like with water, washable clothes and some basic tools can help with the play, though sticks found in the undergrowth work just as well. And of course when back home or in a friend's garden, children love to help out with 'work' in the garden, be that digging or planting and if that turns into making mud pies, well so much the better.

On windy days, children find it very easy to play with the element of air. The wind will stir things up; the feel of it on faces, dry leaves on the ground, leaves on trees, water in a puddle or pond. At the right time of the year, children will pick up handfuls of leaves or dry seeds to send them flying again with the help of a breeze. Bubbles, balloons, wind mills, paper airplanes, home-made or bought kites can all help children actively experience the element that is all around them.

While many people are rightly afraid of fire for the damage it can do, lack of familiarity with this fundamental force can leave children with a

Figure 4.4 Understanding fire

curiosity to play with it as they get older. Evidence suggests that children who experience fire early in their lives learn to appreciate both its creative and destructive qualities. The guidance from the Arson Prevention Bureau[15] is that it is better to help children understand about fire to encourage them to respect it.

It is not often that opportunities to experience fire are present in the public domain. Unlike Northern America and many European countries, most parks in the UK do not provide for outdoor barbeques. Sadly this means that children's experience of fire in public parks is limited to the once-yearly bonfire or fireworks display that some places put on in November. However, like water, fire is still everywhere and children are drawn to the dancing movement within the flames.

There are still lots of opportunities to experience fire in the modern world. As well as using fire in the kitchen, there has been a revival in fire in the home with multifuel stoves and candles used for decoration. Many people have gardens and there is a growing allotment movement meaning that most weekends in the autumn and winter people will be holding an impromptu bonfire. High numbers of playschemes and schools still organize camping trips for children and for some this will be their first experience of the 'reality' of fire. And some young people able to access an adventure playground will experience fire through storytelling or open air cooking over a fire pit.

There has also been more provision for activity weekends by a number of providers across the UK. Typically these involve a two night stay away from home either with a parent or as part of an organized group. The programme will include physical outdoor activity or play.

Case study: Activity weekends and fire

Ben Gold organizes weekends away for groups of fathers and sons or daughters.[16] The events happen near the south coast at an outdoor activity centre ran by the UK Youth Trust and are often attended by people more used to city life, so a no-mobile rule applies over the weekend. The groups stay in well equipped log cabins among the trees that are part of the New Forest. After a shared meal, the group begin by playing a chase game in the dark among the great trees on the estate. It's always young people against parents and the young people always win hands down, but quick friendships are formed that help the weekend run smoothly.

For the two days the group is together they are asked to look after one another and to help in this, a fire is lit at every opportunity. Ben considers the fire to be fundamental to the weekends; it creates a sense of place and a sense of connectedness. People frequently tell stories around a fire and through these learn more about others and themselves. The young people help their fathers collect and chop wood, then tend the fire, and on the Saturday evening cook on an open barbecue learning vital life lessons along the way. The young people tend to self organize, with the more experienced (not always the oldest) showing the others how to keep out of harm. For example, by placing the log seating away from the fire and making sure others walk around the back of anyone seated rather than between them and the fire. The correct way to use a knife is also a vital skill explained during the weekend as all of the participants are encouraged to whittle or carve a piece of wood, using a sharp edge and cutting away from their body.

Other experiences include a choice of outdoor activities such as archery, abseiling, high rope challenges, riding a zip wire, swimming, trust games, kayaking and rafting. Everyone goes on a cross country hike through the New Forest to experience the wide open spaces and the ponies and cattle that live wild there. The weekend finishes with a leaving ceremony where everyone takes a turn to say what was special about the weekend for them. For most, it is clear that something of great import has happened to them and they leave with a greater sense of themselves and a connection to the world around them.

Figure 4.5 Trust games

There has also been a growth in outdoor play in the UK, recognized in play work conferences such as *The Beauty of Play*,[17] *Wild about Play* and the Play Ranger event *Free Range Childhood*.[18] At these events, the value of play outdoors is promoted through direct experience and workshop themes include adventure games, camp-fires, carving, dragon quests, mud sculptures, tree climbing, storytelling and wild walks.

Having looked at the importance of playing actively and outdoors, and how that is good for our bodies, for life skills and for appreciating the natural world, we can also see that it is also good for our self-esteem; the personal feelings created by our minds. The next chapter looks at the different yet interconnected features of playing primarily with internal concepts, ideas and emotions, in our minds, playing intellectually and playing with feelings.

Notes

1. This quote is taken from research (2007) undertaken for this book.
2. Eleanor Goldschmied and Sonia Jackson (1994) *People under Three: Young Children in Day Care* London: Routledge.

3. Desmond Morris (1977) *Manwatching* London: Jonathon Cape.

4. Penny Holland (2003) *We Don't Play with Guns Here: War, Weapon and Superhero Play in the Early Years* Maidenhead: Open University Press. Holland describes how relaxing 'zero tolerance' of war toys and rough and tumble play helps some children play more with their peers.

5. Stephen Biddolph in his book *Raising Boys* (1997) p. 39 quotes research by Robert Rose of the Walter Reed Army Institute of Research. In that study, monkeys were observed to learn about their social structure. Male monkeys were found to have a clear hierarchy based on status. Female monkeys had a looser hierarchy based on factors such as grooming. When a male monkey was given extra testosterone, he became more aggressive and fought his way literally to the top of the tree until the effects of the hormone wore off.

6. Chief Medical Officer (2003) *Health Check: On the State of Public Health* London: Department of Health.

7. Roger Mackett (2004) *Making Children's Lives More Active* University College London: Centre for Transport Studies.

8. Jane Wardle, Naomi Henning Brodersen, Tim Cole, Martin Jarvis and David Boniface (2006) 'Development of adiposity in adolescence'. *British Medical Journal*, (332) 1130–1135.

9. Based on Amelia Lee, Jo A Carter and Xiang Ping (1995) 'Children's conceptions of ability in physical education'. *Journal of Teaching Physical Education*, 14 (4) 384–393.

10. Bob Hughes (1996b) *Play Environments: A Question of Quality* London: Playlink.

11. Edward O Wilson (1986) *Biophilia* Boston: Harvard University Press.

12. Simon Nicholson (1971) 'How not to cheat children: the theory of loose parts'. *Landscape Architecture Quarterly*, 62 (1) 30–34.

13. Find out more about Learning through Landscapes at their website – www.ltl.org.uk/

14. Snug and Outdoor is a company of artists led by sister and brother team Hattie and Tim Coppard; phone: 020 8374 2176 or www.snugandoutdoor.co.uk/index.html

15. The Arson Prevention Bureau has produced a guidance leaflet on Juvenile Fire Setting that is available from the website www.arsonpreventionbureau.org.uk

16. For more information on *Just for Parents* see www.just4parents.co.uk

17. For more information on *The Beauty of Play* Conference see www.ludemos.co.uk

18. For more information on *Wild about Play* and *Free Range Childhood*, contact Playwork Partnerships on 01242 71 4601, email team@playwork.co.uk or www.playwork.co.uk

Playing through feelings and thoughts

5

From before they are born, children are able to perceive the world around them. When they come into the world and grow, children's awarenesses become 'processed' into sights, feelings, sensations, emotions and then thoughts, symbols and ideas. These perceptions do not happen independently of the 'real' world, but neither are they part of it – we can see children running through the world; we cannot see thoughts running through their heads. The experiences we have in the world of shapes inform the world of feelings, and the thoughts we have influence how we behave and act with others. We discussed in the chapter looking at the value of play that early stimulating experiences are critical to brain development, so play in our heads will not fully develop without the corresponding physical play. However once the basic foundations have been built, the mind is capable of creative acts quite independent of any experience in the concrete world. It is our mind that sets us apart from the other mammals.

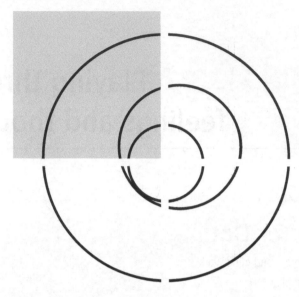

Figure 5.1 Playing through feelings and thoughts

Making wishes come true

We make reality with our minds. And if this is true, then we can also break it with our minds. We can change the way things are by changing our minds about them.

Children do it very easily. In the first few years of life, there are no fixed agreements. Everything has a magical quality. Before minds ossify into the channels prescribed by the current formula, all events are shrouded in mystery. They take place in a world where anything is possible. Objects appear and disappear, the sun rises and sets, people come and go. As a child's mind moves to take all these things into account, it begins to make connections and draw inferences without having access to all the facts. This leads to conclusions which to us seem bizarre and totally delusional. Counting up to twenty while you stand on one leg with your eyes closed is how to make a wish come true. (Lyall Watson 1979)[1]

How the brain and mind work

There is a growing body of opinion that different forms of play are related to different brain functions. Brian Sutton-Smith[2] (building on Gordon Burghardt's work) suggested that play – as we know it – is developed in line with the human brain. Bob Hughes[3] has speculated that the varied forms of play might originate from different parts of the brain. A brief explanation of how we think the brain works will help put these theories into context.

While working at the National Institute of Mental Health, USA in 1968, Dr Paul MacLean put forward the concept of the three-part or triune brain. This idea stated that the brain could be seen as having three distinct regions; the *archiopallium*, a small 'reptilian', primitive brain at the top of the spinal cord, surrounded by the *palaeopallium* or 'old mammalian' limbic brain, which in turn is surrounded by the *neopallium*, or 'new mammalian' neocortex brain. The neocortex is by far the largest part of the human brain taking up two thirds of the total brain mass.[4]

While more modern research[5] tends to support the idea that the brain should be viewed as a whole system, it is still considered valid that the three parts of the brain generally control different functions. The small 'reptilian', primitive brain controls our muscles, balance and basic functions such as breathing and heartbeat; it also influences the basic aspects of behaviour like mating, aggression and anger. The limbic brain is considered to be the chief centre of emotion, attention and affective (emotion-charged) memories. It is made up of four distinct areas – the hippocampus, thalamus, hypothalamus and amygdala that control key bodily functions such as sleep, memory, hormones and behavioural response. The neocortex brain controls the higher thinking functions which distinguish humans from animals. There are many interconnections between the limbic system and the neocortex, so that brain functions should not be considered either purely limbic or purely cortical but a mixture of both; therefore some of what controls our thinking is 'unconscious' or 'preconscious'.

Joseph Le Doux has shown that the amygdala in the limbic system has direct, ultra-fast connections to the eyes and ears that do not involve the conscious brain. The trigger of our 'fight or flight' response is automatic and unconscious – we act on instinct; the response evolving that way to help us respond to attacks as quickly as possible. If we had a brain that routed thoughts to our thinking brain so that we could consider, for example, whether to run away from or fight an attacking bear, it would probably be too late and we'd have been hurt. A different network of structures is described as the 'social brain' and which helps us recognize what others are communicating though body language and emotion. Yet another network is that associated with cognitive development, which is located towards the front of the brain and is one of the slowest parts of the brain to mature,[6] which may explain why we see different forms of behaviour in young children and adolescents. In our lived experience, we are not conscious of these separate parts of the brain; we experience the locus of our thought as our *mind*. This mind, that we feel is responsible for our thoughts and feelings, is formed from the interrelated but distinct regions of the brain resulting in different kinds of thought. These are the basic emotions (anger, fear, happiness, sadness), the secondary emotions (annoyance, dread, pride, despair, guilt, embarrassment to name a few)[7] and then rational, logical thought, which some claim is emotion free – think of 'Mr Spock' from the *Star Trek* science fiction TV/film series.

So how does this affect the different forms of play? Greta Fein (quoted in Brian Sutton-Smith, 2003)[8] recognized that emotion is a strong driver in the play process when she said that play is motivated 'primarily by feelings and not just by images of reality'. Wendy Russell in her work looking at young people who exhibit challenging behaviour[9] quotes Brian Sutton-Smith who suggested that play evolved as a way of mediating the tensions between the different primary and secondary emotional states identified above; the rules, rituals and play signals that identify the behaviour as playing and therefore not 'real' – if we were angry, frightened or sad all the time, the world would be (and is for some) a very hard place to exist. Bob Hughes argues in his book *Play Types: Speculations and Possibilities* that 'the genesis of different play types [might] be located in specific sections of the triune brain'.[10] He suggests a number of possibilities that arise from this speculation. Play types could be categorized as 'basic' play forms that give rise to more complex forms of play. For example, locomotor play (movement) is part of rough and tumble play, but not vice versa. Or play types could be viewed as part of a 'hard to soft spectrum' where for instance play can range from 'hard' (structured or intentional) to 'soft' (unstructured or relaxed). And in an idea that reflects the Integral Play Framework, play types could vary from 'proto-types to mature-types'; each play form has a range or level from very basic to quite complex, the complex form incorporates the basic, but the basic cannot include the complex. So children can walk, toddle and crawl, but babies can only crawl. Young people can manipulate and control the environment (mastery play) yet toddlers can only experiment with it (exploratory play).

Having looked briefly at some thinking on how the brain works and how that may influence our playing, we will now go on to look at the types of play we can experience primarily in our minds.

Awareness

Perceptual play

While not recognized as a form of play in the play types classification, the early, simple acts of newly born babies meet all the criteria of the play cycle. The child has an unconscious desire to engage with a moving object or light source and turn its head or reaches out towards that stimulus. The cycle will be held within a frame made up of the child's perceptual range or physical reach, so will be quite small. The return the child gains from the stimulus will be attractive in proportion to the child's instinctual desires and concentration levels, which again are quite limited in the first few months. Research confirms that very young children shown a rudimentary pattern of three dots on a simple paddle shape will turn towards it and make eye contact. However if the pattern of the three dots is made more 'face-like' with two 'eyes' above a 'mouth', babies will turn towards that pattern in preference to the other shape. Similarly and this is easy to test for yourself, if an adult makes eye contact with a young baby and pokes out their tongue in a playful gesture, the young child will copy and poke out their tongue. The movement may take a little longer than in an older child, but it shows how the child is 'hardwired' to interact with others and the environment. As the child grows these actions move from being solely perceptual and become more impulsive.

Impulsive play

Once children are able to act independently, even when they cannot move independently, they seem driven to explore anything and everything. These actions appear quite spontaneous or impetuous and suggest a transition from purely reactive actions to more directed and focused actions. Impulsive play is where the child acts according to their drives, fascinated by the world around them and wanting to see what they can do to it. Young children will experiment with physical movements, grabbing things; they will try out speech with babbles and coos, they will interact with others through smiles and frowns. These actions are impulsive in that they are not yet fully conscious, nor are they unconscious in the sense of being not cognizant of actions in the world; that is they are beginning to realize that there is a world 'out there', a world that is 'not them'. If we were to see these actions as recapitulative play, we might see the child reliving an early stage of development prior to conscious thinking, what we might describe as a reptilian form of response; acting on basic impulses such as curiosity, hunger, reaction to heat and cold. Impulsive play is part of the 'terrible twos' that most parents experience as the baby becomes a toddler. The child sees everything as touchable, eatable, tasteable, throwable, playful and fascinating. It's not a case of 'act first, think later' – the thinking part of the brain is still in development – it's just action for experience and sensation to feel and see what happens. This form of play overlaps and links into emotional play.

Emotional play

In *Emotional Intelligence*,[11] Daniel Goleman defines emotion as referring to 'a feeling and its distinctive thoughts, psychological and biological states' with their corresponding range of actions. The basic emotions – fear, anger, sadness, enjoyment and love – are the first to emerge and it has been shown[12] that the facial expressions of the first four can be recognized by people worldwide; these are the emotions that children 'know' first. When they grow, as well as exploring how their bodies work, children are beginning to understand and develop the subtle range and boundaries of their emotions. Parents and carers often help children with emerging emotions; think of the games of 'tickle' and peek-a-boo parents play with their children to humour, surprise and 'frighten' the child. At first the use of emotion may be instinctual, though children will quickly come to understand the boundaries around emotion and when to use it to best effect. That understanding will be affected by the use (or loss) of personal will-power, circumstance or the social conditions in which the child grows.

The reason the phrase the 'terrible twos' has emerged to describe young children is that in this period children are often driven by basic emotions and have not yet learned to think about what is happening to them and so their feelings are expressed in the only ways they know how, physically and vocally. Adults often try to explain in words to children what is possible and the children's emotion bursts out in action and expression as they don't yet have the language to respond. And toddlers can often become very frustrated by their incapacity to communicate clearly what their needs are. What parents often see is the 'naughty' act, be that throwing things around, having tantrums or screaming at the top of their lungs.

Children also tune in to the kinds of environment in which to 'experiment'. When children are out with parents and, for example, see something in the supermarket that they want, the emotional and volume ranges are quickly turned up until the parents (usually) give in out of embarrassment. Occasionally it is possible to see the parent who is wise to this game and who 'casually' goes about their business in the dairy aisle while their 3-year-old lies on the floor, shrieking, kicking her feet in an attempt to get a pot of yoghurt. By the way they are treated in response to these outbursts, children often discover how emotion serves them. They also find out what the developing boundaries of behaviour are; as they grow children come to understand the emotional power that they have over others – and the limits of that power. Of course the way we relate to our emotions and the 'control' we have over them are the subject of many books and can only be touched on briefly here. As the Integral Play Framework makes clear, there is an element of emotion in all that we do, so this form of play serves to remind us that children (of all ages) will explore the world of emotion just as they explore the worlds of movement, imagination and relationships.

Imaginative play

Part of Hughes' taxonomy, imaginative play is where the child plays outside the confines of the physical world and plays with things that are not really there or could not really happen. Examples include imagining you are, or pretending to be, a tree or car, or having a friend who isn't there. Sometimes frowned upon by adults who regard it as 'silly', imaginative play has been described by Vivian Gussin Paley (2004) as the *invention of theatre*. She relates this exchange with a young child:

> 'Pretend you're reading Red Riding Hood,' Jilly says, handing me the book.
> 'Not really reading?'
> 'No, pretend you're really reading and I'm really pretending.'[13]

Children are often very aware of the boundaries between the real world and the world of pretend and find it easier to move between those worlds in a moment; moving into the playspace often helps adults flit between and share these worlds with children. The line between pretend and reality is a thin one and adults need to be sensitive in dealing with children playing imaginatively.

> One cannot investigate if one cannot imagine. And one cannot imagine if one does not know. Imagination is limited by experiences, and that includes experiences of the conceptual, the abstract. (Bob Hughes 2001)[14]

Let's pretend

And the world of pretend is where children can try out new roles, new feelings and new possibilities in relative safety. We don't need to provide anything for children to play this way; if anything, all we need to do is not constrain it with disapproving comments or criticism. Imaginative play is important for children. The mind's eye is where children start to become fully human, using the wonder of the human intellect to create things that never were; it's also a way for children to fully appreciate 'otherness'. The things that are 'not me' help create limits to what 'I' am and so help us identify who and what we are.

A healthy dose of imagination is necessary for humans and is a way for us to develop empathy for other people and other creatures, though not all children can develop empathy. Simon Baron-Cohen is a UK-based psychologist who has described those unable to see another person's point of view as experiencing 'mind-blindness'. He believes that this lack of a 'theory of mind' is what results in the condition of autism, where children have difficulties with everyday social interaction, and miss the curiosity of typically developing children.[15] The National Autistic Society estimates that as many as one in a hundred people have some form of autism and research indicates that around four times as many boys as girls are likely to experience autism. Autistic children are also more likely to have difficulty playing with symbols.

Symbolic play

Learning to understand symbols is a critical part of language development but symbols of various types remain important to humans throughout their lives. Symbolic play is related to imaginative play but instead of playing solely in the mind, the 'unreal' representation is extended to an object that stands in for or represents another object. Examples of symbolic play include using a block as a phone, a doll as a child, a cardboard roll as a rocket or fingers to represent a gun. Symbolic play allows children to play 'what if' without any real consequences.

Playing with dolls helps children experience caring for others without risking a living baby; playing with fingers as guns helps children begin to understand about killing and death. The symbol represents something that is not or cannot be present, so it helps support children's investigation of the world and their relationship in it without the risk of them being out of their depth.

Recognizing and using symbols as well as being key to language development is also necessary for creative and representational activities – the drawing of a dog is not a dog; the letters that spell 'd-o-g' are not a dog. Children will create and be drawn to the symbols that hold value for them, whether that value is innate, coming from within or cultural – as Jung said, 'the creative mind plays with the object it loves'. Adults supporting playing children should let the play emerge and develop as it will, for it will help in creating meaning for the child – whether the meaning is known at the start or as it emerges for the child as they play.

Making 'something from nothing'

Creative play adds a different dimension – creativity can be enjoyed for itself or as a means to making something new or responding differently with a known situation. By being creative it is possible that 1 plus 1 may equal 3; something more is created than was there in the constituent parts. The creativity may be in thoughts, in dialogue, in action or in changing objects. We may be creative alone or in groups; most creative activities can be carried out by oneself or in company with others. Creativity may be wholly in the mind such as in creating fantasies, or it may let in others and the world around as in drama or music making (which will be discussed in the next chapter). True creativity comes from within and is enjoyed for its own sake; it is instinctive for children – Picasso said that all children are artists; the problem for many people was how to hold on to creativity as they grew up, how to continue making 'something from nothing'.

Getting serious – deep play

One of the more challenging forms of play is 'deep play' which while involving the body in what may often be risky or potentially life-threatening experiences is really an extreme form of mind play – 'dare I do this or not?' The aim of deep play is not really to die but to experience the thrill of the close encounter, letting us know we are fully alive and so helping conquer our fears. Quite often when adults see children engaging in deep play they may feel compelled to intervene to keep the child safe. This then results in children who may feel unable to take risks on their own terms. We need to understand that taking risks is helpful to children in building up their resilience to the challenges of the world. Deep play may look extreme but is really about understanding the frames or the boundaries – physical and attitudinal (some might even say existential) – that we put around activities.

In a play space, deep play may be climbing to the top of the climbing structure for the first time, holding your breath underwater for as long as possible or riding at high speed through a crowded area. The phenomenon of 'parkour' is an extreme form of deep play, where participants find 'efficient' ways to cross environments, often scaling walls or leaping from balconies high off the ground.[16]

Figure 5.2 Dare I do this?

Most people experience deep play in the fun fair or amusement park where the sensation of taking your life into your hands is offered in a 'safe' environment. Something about the thrill of the fairground causes people to take the rides over and over again. This is how Robert Fulghum, the author of *All I Really Need to Know I Learned in Kindergarten*, explains the sensation:

> It has something to do with risk-taking. Wildness. Adventure. Wanting to break loose from being earth-bound, but safely. Wanting the adrenaline to pump through us in a way that drives home the fact of life and death for a moment. Fear and release. All that, I guess. We didn't consciously think of it that way, but those words point at what we not only wanted, but needed, to happen. (Robert Fulghum 1991 p. 116)[17]

Fulghum is right; we need deep play as it helps us fully experience life. Doing difficult things and overcoming them can be very life affirming and makes us feel good in both body and mind. As adults we might consider abseiling, bungee jumping or parachuting as similar experiences – we know we should not do it but the thrill of success makes it all worthwhile. The actions of deep play will be different for every child; for some it will be jumping off a platform for the first time, going into a dark place without a light or literally going out on a limb on a tree. The point is that as observers we will not really know what is happening inside the child's head till they express it.

Case study: Doing it for yourself

Eleven-year-old Will was halfway through the 'leap of faith' on an outdoor activity session. The 'leap of faith' involved climbing to the top of an erect 10 m timber pole, standing on a small platform at the top before leaping onto a trapeze placed about 3 m away from the pole. Despite the security of the safety harness, this was a challenge for Will and while he had climbed the pole, he found it hard to manoeuvre onto the small platform on the top. Will clung to the top of the pole with all his strength, while his father and friends shouted encouragement from below. The climbing instructor supported Will by letting him know there was no pressure to complete the leap and that he had done well in climbing to the top of the pole; it was Will's choice whether to proceed or climb down. He clung to the pole for nearly 2 minutes, saying 'No' to every suggestion that he climb down. Determined to do it, he finally pushed himself to the little platform, stood up to his full height then made the leap of faith to successfully grab the trapeze. The cheers and support of his friends were outshone by the big smile of satisfaction and achievement he gave as he was lowered back to the ground on his safety line.

Deep play does not always need to be physically life-threatening experiences; as the fear is in the mind it is possible to create a risky, stimulating, fun, dark play space indoors. Turning out the lights and closing the curtains will transform a room into a dark cavern. Weird sounds, smells and textures will then help the mind to move into unknown territory. The party game of 'The Emperor's Eye' may offer ideas. This is where the player is blindfolded and then invited to put their hands into the 'dead emperor's skin' (cold lasagne), his entrails (cold spaghetti) or the emperor's eye (a peeled grape).

Deep play typically will involve children consciously deciding to take a risk, so is usually seen in older children. Of course we recognize that all play is risky at some level if it is new or different so elements of deep play (such as playful fear) may be seen in the activities of quite young children. At a basic level all play involves risk in 'breaking out' of the frames established around our activities; running faster, climbing higher, socializing with a new group, performing a new act. The different types of play are increasingly being recognized as being part of a holistic spectrum that may be present in the play of all children and all adults, so elements of all play types may be present from very early on in the child's play.

All in the mind?

A dominant model in Western education has resulted in the idea that children develop intellectually through key 'ages and stages' and that play is useful in helping children learn the skills necessary in these stages (see Piaget in Chapter 9 'A play history'). However it is now recognized that the key influences on children are many and varied and that children will develop in different ways according to their own experience and desire and the world and people around them. As Lester and Russell expressed it in the summary of their report, *Play for a Change*:

> Contrary to the dominant belief that it is a way of learning specific motor, cognitive or social skills, play has an impact on the architectural foundations of development such as gene expression and physical and chemical development of the brain. In turn, these foundations influence the child's ability to adapt to, survive, thrive in and shape their social and physical environments. Children's development and well-being cannot be understood as separate from their environment. (Lester and Russell 2008a p. 3)[18]

Lester and Russell show through their reviews of many research works that playing influences the physical make-up of the brain. This capacity and ability then helps the child in responding to the experiences and environments they grow up in. As a consequence children who do not have sufficient opportunities to play will experience impaired brain development and flexibility. These conclusions are based on animal studies, though work with extremely deprived children indicates a similar effect.[19]

In this chapter we have looked at how playing supports our feelings and thoughts. The different forms of play each describe activities that involve children using their minds and their bodies to varied degrees. Whatever we believe, it is clear that children need access to a range of playful experiences that they follow according to their own wishes and desires if they are to grow up experiencing their childhood and maximizing their capacity as adults. Some of these experiences will include playing together with other children and adults in creative and culturally specific ways – we will look at these in the next chapter, 'Playing through culture'.

Notes

1. Lyall Watson (1979) in Mick Czuky (Ed.) *How Does It feel?* London: Thames and Hudson p. 258.

2. Brian Sutton-Smith (2003) 'Play as a parody of emotional vulnerability', in Jaipaul L Roopnarine (Ed.) *Play and Educational Theory and Practice, Play and Culture Studies Vol. 5*. Westport, CT: Praeger.

3. Bob Hughes (2006) *Play Types – Speculations and Possibilities* London: London Centre for Playwork Education and Training.

4. Much of this explanation of how the brain works is based on Robert Winston's book (2002) *Human Instinct* London: Bantam Books.

5. Mark H Johnson (2008) *Brain development in childhood: A literature review and synthesis for the Byron Review on the impact of new technologies on children.* Accessed from www.dfes.gov.uk/byronreview/

6. Mark H Johnson (2008) as quoted above.

7. This list is based on Daniel Goleman (1996) *Emotional Intelligence* London: Bloomsbury.

8. Brian Sutton-Smith (1997) *The Ambiguity of Play* London: Harvard University Press p. 157.

9. Wendy Russell and Nottingham City Council (2006) *Reframing Playwork; Reframing Challenging Behaviour* Nottingham City Council.

10. Bob Hughes (2006) as quoted above p. 9.

11. Daniel Goleman (1996) *Emotional Intelligence* as quoted above p. 289.

12. Paul Ekman as reported in Daniel Goleman (1996) *Emotional Intelligence* as quoted earlier p. 290.

13. Vivian Gussin Paley (2004) *A Child's Work: The Importance of Fantasy Play* London: University of Chicago Press p. 20.

14. Bob Hughes (2001) *Evolutionary Playwork and Reflective Analytic Practice* London: Routledge p. 64.

15. Robert Winston (2002) *Human Instinct*, as quoted earlier p. 354.

16. Parkour was developed in the late 1990s by Frenchman David Belle and his friends, who saw the activity as similar to a martial art in its blend of mind and body activity. Parkour gained mainstream attention when it was featured in the opening sequence of the James Bond Film, *Casino Royale* (2006).

17. Robert Fulghum (1991) *Uh-Oh Some Observations from Both Sides of the Refrigerator Door* New York: Ivy Books p. 116.

18. Stuart Lester and Wendy Russell (2008a) *Play for a Change*, Summary briefing published for Play England by the National Children's Bureau p. 3.

19. Stuart Lester and Wendy Russell (2008b) *Play for a Change*, Full report published for Play England by the National Children's Bureau.

Playing through culture

6

When we are playing with thoughts and feelings, a strong element of that play will involve looking at ourselves in comparison to others – specifically those closest to us in our cultural world. Our play will be affected by how we relate to others culturally and creatively. The environment we grow up in and the people around us will affect us as much as the physical nature of our bodies and brains. Our play will involve the signs and symbols used in our environments, the roles that people take, how creative and adaptable they may be, as well as the obvious messages from music, art and drama that surround us.

> No part of culture is innate or biologically transmitted; each and every child is therefore obliged to begin by creating [their] own world image, translating [their] innate biological cognitive 'equipment' into cultural terms. (John Dollard in Cobb 1997 p. 59)[1]

As well as physically exploring the world and thinking things out for themselves, children also make sense of those around them based on the

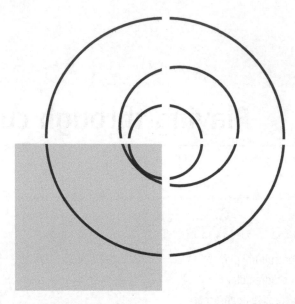

Figure 6.1 Playing through culture

relationships and models they find. At first these influences will be family based; they'll be following mum and dad, granny or close friends, but as the child grows and they get access to TV or start child care or school, other influences will come to bear.

'We liked playing our own little things best; using slop-dosh (mud and water) to decorate Dock leaves, collecting buttons to use like tiddlywinks, and collecting handkerchiefs that we carefully washed and ironed.'[2] Rita was recalling her life in a children's home around 1940. Her reminiscence shows several elements of children's play with others, such as making informal natural 'art', pooling shared items for games and role play, mimicking those around them.

Influences on cultural play

Unlike the genetic code that gives each human two arms, two legs and two eyes, 'culture' – the traditions and values that we are immersed in as we grow – is collected from the people who surround us. Sometimes cultural elements may be very obvious such as the language we use, or the faith our family believes in, but there may also be background elements that have some bearing on how we think of ourselves and others – these may include the schools we go to, the people we play with or the messages we receive from those around us, including the media. For example, in China it was 'traditional' for women who marry to wear red, whereas in the UK it was more 'normal' to wear white. Richard Dawkins termed the 'units of culture' that are passed from one mind to another through conversations or by repeated behaviour *memes*.[3] Examples of memes include traditions or beliefs, or the thoughts that may be seen as 'common sense', or they may be as mundane as advertising jingles or pop songs. Some memes such as neighbourliness and justice may be seen as beneficial; others such as bigotry, sexism and racism will be harmful or destructive. These units of culture vary according to the expectations and common values in the wider community.

Commenting on the perceived differences between girls and boys, Teena Kamen says, 'social conditioning begins from birth, especially the expectations for female and male behaviour'.[4] In an experiment in the 1980s, a baby was dressed in two different sets of clothes and then passed to a series of people who were asked to interact with the baby. In the experiment, the same baby was used, the same environment, with the same type of clothes – the only thing that changed was the colour of the baby's clothes. For one group of people, the clothes were pink, for the other they were blue. What the experimenter found was that the adults treated the baby very differently based on the colour the baby was wearing. When the baby wore pink, the adults commented on how beautiful 'she' was, they held the baby close to their chests and made soft cooing sounds. When the same baby wore blue, the adults said how strong 'he' was, bounced 'him' on their knees and spoke with strong rhythmic sounds. Based on very little evidence, the majority of adults interacted with the baby as if it were a girl when wearing pink and a boy when wearing blue. The adults assumed the gender of the child and treated it accordingly to the norms of that gender. Interestingly, Jo Paoletti has shown that pink for girls has only been a dominant colour in the West since the Second World War. Paoletti stated that prior to that period, blue was the preferred colour for girls as it was 'more delicate and dainty'.[5] What is clear is that as they learn the language of the community they are raised in, children will learn the symbols and values of that community, whether expressed consciously or unconsciously by family members.

Children's play will be influenced by these cultural elements, these memes, whether they are subtle or obvious. For example, in the UK and

USA, the group combat game 'Cowboys and Indians', popular in the 1950s and 1960s due to the influence of magazines and films, is identical in play to 'Power Rangers', a TV series first broadcast in 1993. Both games involve a battle between 'good and evil' – though of course which side is which is culturally determined by the players (or more often by adults if they feel inclined to intervene in the play). And though it cannot be proven, it is probable that children used to play a similar game called 'Greeks and Barbarians' over 3,000 years ago.

Games that children play

In 1959 the playground games that children played were recorded by Iona and Peter Opie in the classic text *The Lore and Language of Schoolchildren*.[6] That well-researched work showed the amazing variety of pastimes, games and riddles that children got up to when adults were not watching. It also confirmed that while many of the games played would be recognized UK wide (even worldwide), the regional varieties were influenced by local conditions and increasingly by films and magazines. Forty years after the Opies did their work, adults began to question if children still knew how to play. David Rowan writing in the *Times Magazine*[7] found that, contrary to the opinions of the adults nearby, children's playground cultures were still strong with games and rhymes. In a 2005 interview with a then 81-year-old Iona Opie, Rowan reports her as saying that children will always need 'a ritualized means of confronting social anxieties, affirming their growing independence, or simply channelling their aggression or sexual curiosity' through games and rhymes. To prove the point, Rowan went into playgrounds and collected some of the current chasing and rhyme games; here's an example from a primary school child in Glasgow, which has a variety of old and modern influences and also highlights the lack of innocence in children's games:

> Jingle bells, jingle bells, Santa's lying dead.
> Teletubbies Teletubbies stabbed him in his head.
> Barbie girl, Barbie girl tried to save his life.
> Action Man, Action Man stabbed him wi' a knife...[8]

Children frequently explore things in their play that well-meaning adults might disapprove of: toilet humour, profanity, sex roles, sex parts and violence. Many youngsters pass through a phase of giggling hysterically when the words 'poo' or 'willy' are mentioned; many teenagers use rude language when with their friends that they would not use at home. This is all part of playing with the cultural frames around our behaviour; we only find out the edge of the frame when we have gone 'too far'. Play is a safer way of exploring these issues between people and finding out the 'tribal norms'.

Stories may also help children find out about cultural themes such as good and evil, right and wrong, love and jealousy. Folk tales and 'fairy stories' reveal some of life's secrets for children through the images and symbols used. These symbols often have more meaning for younger children than the factual, intellectual meanings they may carry. Children can identify with the small piglets being chased by the larger wolf, who by combining their resources and ideas eventually overcome the threat and 'live happily ever after'. A reassuring story perhaps for little people surrounded by those much bigger (and sometimes hairier) than themselves.

Stories that children tell

Left to their own devices, children can also make up their own stories – with the power of creativity and imagination, they can make the wingless take flight and the dead come alive. Children naturally have this ability whereas adults often need reminding of the magic that is all around them. Some adults believe in brutal honesty with children, discouraging creative or fantasy play and only admitting to the 'reality' of the objective world – 'there are no such things as fairies or monsters under the bed'. But all cultures have their folk tales with heroes and villains that serve as a way to focus imaginations and carry cultural messages. Most parents recognize that the best way to proceed is in supporting children's ideas, until the 'truth' is discovered in their own time (e.g. Santa doesn't squeeze down the chimney on Christmas Eve).

Activity: Telling tales

Story-making can be a wonderful way for children to discover the power of creativity and imagination. Some children spontaneously love telling stories and playing with characters, others need a little support to play with stories. There are many ways to help start the creative process.

Activity—cont'd

Working in a group and using a few simple rules, a story circle can quickly generate funny or heroic stories. A volunteer starts the story with a lead character and a situation – 'Once upon a time, there was a foolish wizard who only had three spells left in his magic box. One day he received a summons from the queen so he…' The first teller then ends the tale on a suspense point for it to be picked up by the next person and so on until a natural ending is reached.

Another way, particularly useful outdoors, if the children are willing, is to ask them to find a piece of land that attracts them in some way. Once they have found a piece of land, ask them to describe it and the creatures that live on it. When all the children have found their voices through description, ask them to create a situation for the ones who live on the land; stories often emerge quite naturally, though a final stage could be to pair up two children and two sets of 'inhabitants' to see how the two worlds and situations intercept.[9]

Or you could use a story basket, an assorted mix of objects from which children draw three at random and try to make a story from what they find. The stories may be stand alone or they may build on one another much as in the story circle. Examples of objects to put in the basket (or box or bag) include keys, stones, feathers, spoons, coins, material, rings – whatever is to hand or can be found in the natural environment.

Playful and creative approaches

As discussed in 'Playing through feelings and thoughts', children are innately creative; though sadly well-meaning but didactic adults can result in children 'learning' what is expected from artistic activities. All too often these days, children are expected to get it right first time and produce a successful picture from the first draft. Consequently some children's settings offer 'colour by numbers' images for children to fill in to show their parents at the end of the day. But these deny children's natural creativity and instead teach them to follow patterns. Over time children may lose their confidence in creating and only 'deliver' what is expected; for example all trees have brown trunks with green bushy leaves, all cats have rounds heads and round bodies.

A different approach is in the Reggio Emilia region of Italy, where young children are supported to find their 'hundred languages' of expression, where it is believed that children have 'a hundred hands, a hundred thoughts, a hundred ways of thinking of playing, of speaking'.[10] In this

Figure 6.2 Being creative

system, a playful and creative approach is taken to the education and care of young children. The creativity of children as young as 3 and 4 is supported through encouraging natural observation and without barriers or expectations so that the children produce paintings, drawings and artworks of tremendous clarity and passion. This approach for the education of young children is being adopted and promoted throughout the UK and elsewhere across the world. It has yet to be seen how long lasting the effects will be in these different contexts.

Being playfully creative helps develop children who are curious about the nature of ideas and materials, flexible in the way they use those ideas and materials, persistent in finding new responses and new connections, and overall develops children's confidence in their thinking. Key to supporting creativity is recognizing that experimenting is risky; things don't always turn out as planned. As Edward de Bono said, 'It is better to have enough ideas for some of them to be wrong, than to be always right by having no ideas at all.'

Activity: Supporting creativity in a play setting

Creative arts and crafts play can be supported with simple materials: water and things to mix in it, sand and things to shape it, scrap paper, pencils, crayons, old clothes, in fact 'junk' of any kind.

First of all, trust in children's inherent creative drive; support that by providing an environment with lots of material for making and adapting. Try not to be judgemental with what is produced; remember it's for the child to decide where the work starts and ends. Don't look for a finished product and don't put works on display unless the child asks you.

Children can play games with creativity such as taking a line for walk, making a mark on a paper then passing it to another person for them to extend or complete. Repeat as often as the children feel is necessary.

Once the 'artists' are happy making marks, they could draw round their hand. Then turn the image round till they feel inspired to make another image from what they originally drew. The randomness of the hand image can often be a springboard for wildly creative images.

Encourage playing with mark making. Using whatever materials are to hand – pencils, pens, paint, ink, mud, spices in a little water (e.g. ground cayenne, cumin, or turmeric) – support haphazard mark making for the children to rediscover randomness and spontaneity. This can be fun in itself but over time the children might start using the marks to create their own images. The point is to offer other ways to make images than traditional line drawing with precise outlines or patterns.

If you are outdoors, ask the children to find a space that is attractive to them. Ask them to think of the colours, the patterns, the contrasts in the space; what can they see or what's missing (negative shapes). Look for materials in the space (leaves, twigs, mud, sand, stones, snow and ice) and make an image, pattern or sculpture from what they find.[11] The artworks of Andy Goldsworthy, who works with leaves, petals, twigs, mud, snow, water and pebbles, may be useful for inspiring you or the children to make something from what you find.

It is also amazing what 'waste' cardboard can do. Many children find cardboard boxes a wonderful play cue and can spend hours finding things to do in, on and with the box. Boxes can be taken apart and used as large canvases for art works, or as road plans for games with wheeled toys. They may also be used much like large building bricks and stuck together using parcel tape to create dens or castles or rocket ships, or whatever.

Creativity in children doesn't have to involve much material or preparation; they will use the materials and opportunities around them to explore pattern and shape. Small children will use food to make patterns on the surfaces around them; on sunny days older children might use water bottles to make patterns on hot pavements. Young people might turn their creativity into the (sometimes socially challenging) activity of graffiti, where aerosol paint is used to create 'works of art' – or 'vandalism' – depending on the point of view of the observer.

What's real?

Symbolic play in the mind was discussed in the previous chapter, but symbols may also be representative of the cultures we play in. A symbol is something that stands for or represents something else; so children using stones as animals in their play is an example of symbolic play. While 'not real' the stone animals will tend to be from the child's world; so for children growing up in a rural setting they may represent farm animals and children with access to a TV or a zoo may play with more exotic animals such as lions and giraffes. The point is that the symbol stands for the real thing so allows children to play with and explore things in their world without losing control – playing with real animals might be too challenging or frightening. Similarly making daisy chains as necklaces or bottle tops into coins helps the child play with 'precious' objects that might be out of reach in their day-to-day world. Sara Smilansky, after doing research with disadvantaged children, concluded that the quality of children's dramatic and symbolic play was affected by background cultural influences. Smilansky found that this difference, rather than being caused by cognitive factors as other theorists have argued, was better explained by the cultural and socialization processes enveloping the children; those with limited 'information' tended to have more limited 'materials' to play with.[12]

Play with roles

Children also love play that helps them understand and explore different cultural roles. These roles might be as their parents or carers, as teachers or police officers, as gangsters or criminals or others in their lives. Playing with roles can be fun and can also help children comprehend the diversity and complexity of roles – good mom, bad mom; bad teacher, kind old man. While these might not be strictly 'accurate' roles in the sense of mimicry, they may be archetypal and help children explore what it might be like to be in these roles.

Role models and archetypes

Archetypes are the fundamental roles that frequently describe the 'typical' characters that we might come onto contact with. Each character is capable

Figure 6.3 Playing with monsters

of a light and dark side, for instance, playing the 'joker' can help people see the funny side of life or it could be a way of concealing emotions. Mothers can be supportive and nurturing, or smothering and clinging, fathers may be positive role models or authoritative and dictatorial. While children may not always comprehend the depth of a role, they recognize the fact that it is a role and one that they can comply with or challenge; as they will at different places in their life. Playing roles helps children relate to others and understand that most roles are culturally and contextually determined – the same person can act differently in different places in their life.

Role models and archetypes will be different in diverse cultures; but the underlying messages will be very similar, examples include stories from Robin Hood, the Monkey King of China or *Star Wars*. In all these stories, there are good and bad people, people who help or hinder the hero or heroine, a journey to be taken, a wrong to be righted and a prize to be won.

Dramatic play

This form of play takes role play further and puts it in a particular frame or setting, usually of the children's construction (we are talking here about a metaphysical frame rather than a literal one, though that might be involved). Dramatic play is different to role play in that it dramatizes events of which the child may have no direct experience. Basically children enjoy pretending to be others and performing in front of friends and family, whether that is in a game, in a formal show, as characters from a pop video, or more recently, pretending they are part of TV programmes *Pop Idol* or *X-Factor*, complete with dancers and judges. This creative role play can be supported with masks, face paints, a box of costumes, a music player or even a karaoke machine. Children might take the play further and improvise a musical, using popular songs as a start and adapting their own lyrics.

The drama may take a more serious tone and use elements of a sacred or celebratory event, such as getting married or even a funeral. Whatever the form of the play, adults should let the drama take its course. As is made clear in the *Playwork Principles*, 'the children and young people determine and control the content and intent of their play, by following their own instincts, ideas and interests, in their own way for their own reasons'.[13]

Eloise was playing in her after school club, and had collected half a dozen dolls to play with. Working quietly and carefully, she removed the dolls' heads from their bodies and lined them up in a row. The adults in the setting were observing and whispering concerns one to the other, worried that this might indicate some underlying behavioural problem. When Eloise's mother arrived to collect her, one of the staff reported Eloise's behaviour to her, whereupon the mother explained that the night before they had seen a video of *Buffy the Vampire Slayer*. The story-line had involved just such a scene and Eloise was replaying the story with her dolls.[14]

If adults are working to support children in their play, it is useful to be aware that different stories will be played by children. Adults should try to not direct them or decide on the ending, but rather allow the children's story to go where they want it to. Daniel Goleman tells how after incidents in their lives, children will often use role play and dramatic play to 'work out' the meaning of the incident for themselves.[15] Goleman gives examples of how children might make games around extreme trauma, but children may also be playing out a recent holiday, a sports day – or the funeral of a relative; we need to support these activities and resist the temptation to make everything, 'happy ever after'.

CS Lewis, the author of the well-loved *Chronicles of Narnia*, was commenting about stories for children, but the message he gave was very clear and relevant to this type of play and adults' reaction to it:

> Those who say that children must not be frightened may mean two things. They may mean (1) that we must not do anything likely to give the child those haunting, disabling, pathological fears against which ordinary courage is helpless: in fact, *phobias*... Or they may mean (2) that we must try to keep out of his mind the knowledge that he is born into a world of death, violence, wounds, adventure, heroism and cowardice, good and evil. If they mean the first I agree with them, but not if they mean the second. The second would indeed be to give children a false impression and feed them on escapism in the bad sense... Since it is so likely that they will meet cruel enemies, let them at least have heard of brave knights and heroic courage. Otherwise you are making their destiny not brighter but darker. (Lewis 1982 p. 778)[16]

The nature of play is not always fun and frivolous; it can have a 'dark' side that some adults may find challenging. This is a difficult issue as adults may find some play confrontational, rude, offensive or prejudiced. Adults should be cautious about intervening in children's playing, for by changing or stopping the play, its meaning will be changed and the drama loses its force. Keeping children in a world where nothing bad ever happens will disadvantage them as they grow older; they'll be more shocked when reality intrudes. This is not a request that all children are introduced to the horrors of the world as soon as they can walk, but it is to ask that when they show they are ready to enquire about such things that we give a mature response. It is when we affect their thinking by offering our own perspectives and prejudices as the 'truth' of a situation that we risk doing the greatest harm. Children need to be offered breadth and depth in the responses from the adults around them if they are to be best able to make sense of the dramas in their world. Our responses need to be emotionally mature and as authentic as we can make them, showing respect for the child and their thoughts.

Fantasy play

Fantasy play sits on the border between mind play and cultural play; it is a play where the child takes on elements of a world different from the reality we inhabit. The play helps children explore the nature of reality and unreality in a non-threatening and so helpful way. The word 'fantasy' means dreamlike, unreal, invented; to be 'fantastic' is to be out of this world or unbelievable. This type of play might include a role that is not real ('Power Ranger'), powers not manifest (flight) or places we can't normally visit (the moon). Fantasy play is always of the child's making (if not then it's 'acting'), though may be negotiated with others. It may be very much in the child's head, needing no script or costume, but is also part of the child's interaction with others. 'Pretend you're dead', says one child; 'No, I don't want to be', replies the other. 'Ok', says the first, 'But pretend you're a zombie so I can chase you.' 'Ok', says the second and the play is on. Part of 'growing up' is beginning to understand the difference between the internal and external realities and the limits to what we can do as individuals.

Recapitulative play

The last form of cultural play to be described in this chapter is recapitulative play, where a child's play 'recapitulates' or runs through the stages that humankind has gone through in our evolution. Examples of this might be: chasing others for food or self-preservation, den building, using weapons, domesticating and looking after other animals, going to war, building civilizations. In describing this form of play, Hughes states that the concept has not always been received positively due to assumptions that it was linked to 'ideal' forms of human development; that is, if you did not play in certain ways you were 'less evolved' than others. However, Hughes puts the concept succinctly as, 'if you look at some of what children do when they play, you will see reflected in that, some of what human beings did in the ancient past'.[17] He also states that this form of play is common to children the world over whatever their cultural or racial background.

Recapitulative play is considered evolutionary in that the forms of play will have developed and been strengthened by natural selection, so those forms of play that lended an advantage will have been favoured. Many aspects of recapitulative play such as those forms of play listed above would be challenging in many modern settings. If we add in fire making, ritualistic play, mask making and body decoration, we quickly create a list of 'do nots' for many children's settings. However when we recognize that these forms of play impart essential human and life skills, we begin to see the need to ensure that children do not miss out on this kind of opportunity.

Case study: 'Five dangerous things you should let your kids do'

Gever Tulley is the co-founder of the Tinkering School, a week-long camp for children ran over the summer break from normal school. Tulley encourages children in the Tinkering School to 'play' with power tools, to build their own bridges using only timber poles and string and make model boats from waste materials.

In a recent online presentation,[18] Tulley (2007) suggested, 'Five dangerous things you should let your kids do'. These included playing with fire, owning and using a pocket knife, throwing a spear, deconstructing modern appliances and breaking rules, such as driving off road without a driving licence. Tulley's aim with these activities was not for them to be dangerous, but for them to give children new skills and new ways of looking at the world – children learn things playing with fire that they don't get from a cooker hob; they get a different experience taking a washing machine apart than they do from playing with building bricks. Despite the modern focus of the Tinkering School, there is a good link to recapitulative play: the first three activities – playing with fire, using a knife, throwing a spear – are things that children would have been doing as part of growing up for over 10,000 years. Tulley argues that giving children the chance to explore in this playful way will make them stronger and smarter and so less susceptible to danger in the long run.

Rituals and play

Despite the fact that recapitulative play contains many elements of other forms of play (such as running around, using subtle and obvious skills, taking risks and playing with identity), it has been discussed in this chapter on cultural forms of play, as many of its attributes suggested a genetic or mimetic transition from generation to generation; it's either in our genes or we learn it from others around us. Many of these forms of play are suggestive of 'rites of passage' for children; as we discussed in Chapter 4 'Playing actively', the first times children struck a match, cooked outdoors, went on a midnight walk, or buried a pet have significant and usually positive impacts on children that they remember for a long time. In an adult dominated and 'safe' environment, where their activities are controlled or prescribed, children are often denied these opportunities and so lose out.

In our wider cultures, we understand that rituals are an important part of coming to terms with change, be that in gaining something, as in births or marriages, or losing something such as in separation or death. Rituals are just as important to children; they may be 'playing' at getting married or having a baby, but the experiences will be valid and important in helping children find their ways through life.

Play spaces can sometimes be the only spaces that children can use to express their feelings. In *Making Sense: Playwork in Practice*, the story is told of two children whose father had recently died.[19] The children 'took over' a tyre swing on a playground that they made their own for a time. In their grief, they needed a place to come to terms with what had happened. Other children respected their space and left them alone in their reverie. After a few days, the children began to rejoin the normal life of the play site. No-one can really know what was going on for the children, but the need they had was apparent and the sympathetic space was given over for them to work through this event in their lives.

In this chapter we have looked at the value of play in contributing to how children associate with others. We've seen how the influences of others' beliefs and opinions may affect how children play and the choices they have to conform with or challenge those cultural values. Different forms of play have been discussed looking at the ways they help children explore their relationships with others and so shape an individual idea of who they are themselves. In the next section, we'll look at how we connect to others in a material, social sense; how roles and status between humans impact on play.

Notes

1. John Dollard as quoted by Edith Cobb (1977) *The Ecology of Imagination in Childhood* Dallas: Spring Publications p. 59.
2. This quote was taken from research undertaken for this book.
3. Richard Dawkins (1989) *The Selfish Gene* Oxford: Oxford University Press.
4. Teena Kamen (2005) *The Playworker's Handbook* London: Hodder Arnold p. 204.
5. Jo Paoletti (no date) *Dressing for Sexes* online accessed 12 July 2008 from www.gentlebirth.org/archives/pinkblue.html
6. Iona and Peter Opie (1959) *The Lore and Language of Schoolchildren* Oxford: Oxford University Press.
7. David Rowan (21 May 2005) 'Have children really forgotten how to play?' *The Times Magazine* online accessed 11 June 2007 from www.davidrowan.com
8. David Rowan (21 May 2005) as above. Rowan's website includes many more examples both playful and physically or sexually violent.
9. This approach is an adaptation of that used by storyteller Jane Flood.
10. Extract from a poem by Loris Malaguzzi, co-founder of the Reggio Emilia system of education and care for children in Italy.

11. For more ideas on what to play with outdoors, look at *Nature's Playground* by Fiona Danks and Jo Schofield (2005) published in London by Frances Lincoln Ltd.

12. Sara Smilansky (1968) *The Effects of Sociodramatic Play on Disadvantaged Preschool Children* New York: Wiley.

13. The *Playwork Principles* create a professional and ethical framework for playwork. Written by the Playwork Principles Scrutiny Group in 2005, there are eight 'principles' that as it says in the framework's introduction, 'describe what is unique about play and playwork, and provide the playwork perspective for working with children and young people'. See Play Wales' website for more information on the Principles: www.playwales.org.uk/page.asp?id=50

14. *Buffy the Vampire Slayer,* a television series about a teenage vampire killer, was created by Joss Whedon. The episode involving dolls heads was called 'The Witch' and was first broadcast 17 March 1997.

15. Daniel Goleman (1996) *Emotional Intelligence* London: Bloomsbury p. 208.

16. CS Lewis (1982) 'On three ways of writing for children' from *On Stories and Other Essays on Literature* London: Harcourt. Reprinted (2004) in *Chronicles of Narnia* London: Harper Collins p. 778.

17. Bob Hughes (2006) *Play Types – Speculations and Possibilities* London: London Centre for Playwork Education and Training pp. 50–51.

18. Gever Tulley's presentation, *5 dangerous things you should let your kids do*, is available from www.ted.com

19. Playlink (2001) *Making Sense: Playwork in Practice* London: Playlink p. 15. This book contains many real-life play stories that aim to help people understand the nature of playwork. The stories are given in some detail and then the benefits of the activities are mapped out using various quality standards.

Playing with others

Chapter Outline

Children's interactions are not preparation for life; they are life itself.

Barrie Thorne (1993 p. 3)[1]

It's vital to our lives as gregarious, sociable animals that we play and get on with others. We have a shared experience of values and beliefs with other humans and we have a social world of roles and relationships with others. Social expectations impact on children both positively and negatively from the day they are born, with some adults affording children lots of choice in what they do and how they play and others very little. Babies' first experiences of others are with those looking after them in the immediate family circle, and as they grow this circle widens to include friends, neighbours, then strangers both in the home and school situation. Different forms of play help us explore our roles and relationships in this changing world. Children and young people are beginning to be consulted in the matters that affect their lives.

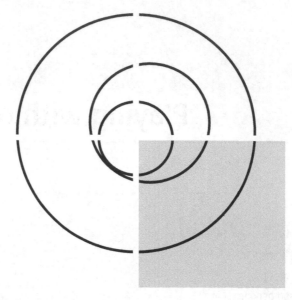

Figure 7.1 Playing with others

Built a tent house for the girls in their bedroom. Darla [age 4]: 'Now you be the daddy and I'll be the mummy and you be the big bad wolf. No. I be the mummy and Irial [older sister] be the little baby...' etc.
  Her establishing all the relationships is actually the game. Nothing much else happens – we just sort out the kinship rules. Must be a deep tribal gene manifesting. (Brian Eno 1994)[2]

Children quickly grasp the concept of roles: who's leading, who's following and who's got the power. In games, this can be explored to find out who is the 'top dog' – the origin of this phrase is quite deliberate; the top dog is the one in control. Status may be explored through roles (as in the example given by Eno), language, skills or strength trials – or a combination of these.

Playing at home

Children's first playmates are their immediate family, with whom as well as playing their first games they will also find out about their changing status in the family. As has been discussed, mothers and fathers may interact with the child to 'bond' with them, though once children start becoming independent, parents will often leave them to their own devices. Every child will have a slightly different experience in the home setting, and there is plenty of evidence that a positive home environment offers children the best start in life as was discussed in 'Playing through feelings and thoughts'. However research into family play in different societies reveals clear generic patterns. Some societies believe in playing with their children; others do not play, or do so to varying degrees.[3] Many British, North American and Chinese mothers see themselves as playmates for their children, setting aside time and joining in with their play. However Mexican, Italian and Korean families generally do not consider play to be important for children's development, so play at home is supported by siblings, other family members or neighbours if at all. Additionally whatever the background of the family, if other pressures are affecting the family, there may be no time or resources for play; if the adults are working hard to make a living and care for their children, they may not consider play at all. These early experiences will help shape children's ideas about how to relate to others through play. The varied reactions from those around will result in children who play with their parents, play with brothers and sisters or make their own play in the opportunities they have.

Playing in groups

The differences in 'what is normal' for play may cause difficulties for children or practitioners when children begin to use provision. If the children are used to making their own play, they may not understand when the adults try to lead or facilitate the play. And if children are used to adults acting as playmates, they may be waiting for the cue to play before getting started themselves, not being used to initiating the play themselves. When with other children and adults, play extends into the social arena, either playing directly with others, parallel to them or not with them at all. The practitioners will need to be sensitive to the children's needs if they are not to intervene incorrectly; however, other children may not be so sensitive.

For example, the practitioners in a 'special school' used board games to help social interactions between the children with varied needs in the setting. The children, who could be violent either verbally or physically, would often not play well with others who they saw as different or strange (aren't we all

Figure 7.2 Playing with others

different or strange to each other?). The staff introduced board games to help the children interact with each other. Intuitively they recognized that the rules of the board game would help mimic the rules needed to function in shared society. The playful approach was not threatening in a way that more formal approaches could have been for these children. The children responded well to the play frame created by the board game; they understood that behaviour in the frame was different to behaviour outside. Over time game rules were introduced to help the children make the connection between their behaviour and the consequences of their actions. For instance in the game of Monopoly™, a fine was introduced for young people who swore; £10 was put into 'Free Parking' for every transgression. The game then revolved around catching out the others who were swearing, and trying hard not to pay excessive fines oneself.

The individual child's perspective of playing in groups may be affected if the child has extra differences to the other children, such as ability, language or skill. Professor Paul Gately has done a lot of work with overweight children and runs camps to help children manage their weight.[4] Gately knows that overweight children may be isolated within groups as they are often unable to join in the play with others, either for physical reasons or because they may be bullied by the others due to their appearance. He recognizes that in order to help obese or overweight children, he needs to work on their exercise levels and dietary intake, but also with their friendship groups and families to help change lifestyles and so increase the child's self-confidence and self-esteem. Gately puts great store by the social atmosphere generated within his 'fat camps' and a playful yet scientific approach is taken which includes everyone. His work has been recognized worldwide for the long lasting effects it has on children's health.

Even when children are able to play together things do not always go smoothly; there is still a need for negotiation and compromise. When children want to play with others, the play cues issued do not always match the first time around. One child tries to assert their authority by setting the rules of the game; the other child refuses to play as it feels 'unfair'. The first child offers an alternative, the second says, 'OK then' and the play cycle is formed. Asbjørn Flemmen describes this compromise as 'the pre-school of democracy...OK then – the two most important words in the language'.[5] Playing together gives children an awareness of authority, as well as all the other benefits it brings – it may only be fleeting or it may continue through the play and into their longer term relationships. Through playing with others, children find out about negotiation and compromise, about leading and following – and about anarchy.

Case study: Swimming pool

It was the last weekend of the summer school holiday and we went with friends to a traditional park playground in a small country town. There was a swimming pool full of children, glowing in the summer sun.

Our four children played there for an hour while we watched and chatted. About 40 different children used the pool, all ages, between 12 months and 14 years, 25 per cent girls, 75 per cent boys. For most, the pool was an impromptu play space, as they were wearing nothing or underwear rather than swim suits.

In that hour, most of the children guided their own play, paddling, splashing just for the fun of it, splashing each other and occasionally the audience, playing with the fountain, chasing each other round the pool or playfighting. For most of the time, all the children were left to their own devices by the parents. The exceptions were the young toddlers who were helped into the pool and occasionally shepherded around

Case study—cont'd

it. The children tended to form into groups for their play, mostly with others with whom they had come to the pool. Occasionally they made new friendships in the splashing games until their parents took them away, usually because they had been in the water too long and were beginning to shiver, or because it was time for tea.

In all that time, some parents found it necessary to warn other children about their boisterous behaviour on about six occasions. Some of the splashing went over the toddlers; the culprits always modified their behaviour and sometimes apologized. A group of 3 boys of around 12 dominated the pool for about 10 minutes during which time they knocked over a smaller boy of 6 years. There were several shouts and they immediately stopped what they were doing and started another game, which appeared to involve trying to pull off each other's shorts and/or push the other's head under the water. However, for most of the time, the children played within the boundaries they understood to be acceptable for the space, the numbers present and the ages nearby.

As the swimming pool case study shows, children left to their own devices can often manage their own behaviour in relation to many other children of different abilities and ages. The play opportunity created with the pool invited a certain type of activity which often involved playing with the water and splashing others. There was much good natured play within and across age groups, with lots of informal negotiation and compromise in the use of spaces and water. When the activity went too far for some, the cues and responses indicated that and the activity was curtailed or amended. On the one occasion, the larger boys went too far, and the real 'top dogs' – the adults – intervened to reset the boundaries. No adult guided the play for the majority of the children, no rules were posted on the wall for all to obey, and no regulations governed the numbers of children and what they could get up to in the play space. No doubt some of the playful behaviour would have been curtailed had it happened in some play provision; it was far too 'violent', but no-one was seriously hurt by any other child and most of the children appeared to be enjoying the activity, the majority having fun.

Playfighting

The physical aspect of rough and tumble play was discussed in 'Playing actively', yet this form of play also has a strong social element. As well as testing physical boundaries, rough and tumble is about social boundaries, understanding closeness and distance – the end of the physical play is often with a pile of children laughing while they sat on one another. In play, the roles may change so that the one who is in charge while the others follow only lasts a short time before the roles reverse. The relationships formed in the 'fight' can continue with extended rapport and attachments long afterwards.[6] Typically boys will engage in obvious playfighting and rough and tumble play, but girls' group play can also be competitive. With girls it tends to be expressed emotionally and through language rather than physically; perhaps by arguing about who should take what role in their games; and like boys occasionally it can go too far and individuals get hurt. It is well understood that girls can be competitive in terms of appearance and dress, and may be quite critical of those not in the gang. Not surprisingly, there are always children who will challenge these stereotypes – 'tomboys' who love to run wild, joining in the rough play and boys who prefer to play more sedentary games and avoid playfights and team games like cricket or football.

Children and gender

A lot has been written about the differences and similarities in gender and how adult expectations may impact on play relationships between boys and girls. Studies into gender play have been extensive and cover a variety of ages across a number of countries and contexts.[7] Relevant to this section on social play is the power relationship between girls and boys in their play. Commentators often state that typically boys tend to have more space in which to play and can dominate spaces and intrude into girls' space and play forms. Observations of most playgrounds will usually show the boys running around playing chase or ball games, whereas the girls will be in smaller groups, usually less active. And interestingly while boys can intrude on girls' space, they rarely play the girls' games, though girls, while not breaking into boys' space, find it easier to join in their play. The reasons for this are many and varied, being based on a number of genetic, physical, cultural and social factors. However it is a truism that girls tend to have less choice in their free play and there is evidence that girls' play is supported in staffed provision where the extremes of boys' play are curtailed.[8]

While most settings (and some parents) would plan to be 'gender neutral' and offer positive images in their support for children and their play, the reality is that children are individuals within a variety of contexts and their social

Figure 7.3 Climbing trees together

and gender relationships are shaped by their responses to those contexts. Children carry with them the experiences they have found in other places and with other people, children and adult. While many of the play types discussed here are innate and engagement with them child initiated, social and cultural circumstances will influence the child's assimilation and expression of those play types, some being stronger and more accomplished, others less so. We should recognize that children are active in this process and very able to make their own decisions when given information and alternatives; being aware of this will help adults offer an authentic response to support the child's play.

Communication play

Gregory Bateson, a North American anthropologist, considered play to be an important step in the evolution of communication, for in play the signals stand for other things than themselves – there is an element of symbolic representation, the play cues telling the other that 'this is play'.[9] This is very evident in communication play where the interaction is around the forms of

communication itself: how things are said, what is said and the body language involved.

This kind of play may involve only gestures and no spoken words, often
done by children to challenge those in authority in situations where they are
expected to behave (say in church or in school). They might mime to one
another, acting out a ridiculous scenario or simply passing messages. At other
times the play may be on voice tone or include a mismatch of what is said
with how it is said. The comic actor Peter Kay frequently draws on memories
of children's play to great effect in his stage shows, where he uses a variety of
gestures, voices and actions to indicate how his real message may be the very
opposite of what is apparently communicated. The audience read his irony,
play-acting and teasing as humorous rather than cruel or malicious.

Communication play can also involve playing with words, as in mixing
parts of words up ('pixing marts of up words') or using them out of context
('As Bob is my witless'),[10] telling jokes or making up nonsense rhymes and
limericks. These examples of jokes from children attending a holiday playscheme in Sheffield rely on knowledge of words and meanings to work:

Q: How do chickens wake up in the morning?
A: With an alarm cluck

Stephanie aged 9

Q: Why did the cow cross the road?
A: To go to the moo-vies
Q: Where do sheep go on holiday?
A: Baa aa celona

Salah aged 12

Many of the street rhymes collected by the Opies (as discussed in the previous chapter) involve playing with the structure and sound of the rhyme.
Often the rhymes would take a known and therefore expected ending in a
new direction:

Mary, Mary, quite contrary.
How does your garden grow?
I live in a flat, you stupid prat,
So how the heck should I know?![11]

Playing with words and language is about with rules and boundaries,
norms are challenged and new ways of doing things explored. Children
know that they can use different language with friends than they can with

most adults; peer-to-peer language might be more sexual or use street slang. Arguing, debating and 'banter' take the play to another level, but usually only between peers; as with all forms of social play, an imbalance in abilities often leads to an imbalance in power and so may result in behaviour that may be experienced as bullying.

Communication play relies on an ability to play with communication norms, such as open dialogue, eye contact, appropriate body language and engaged listening. There is growing concern, reported through the media, that some children are not involved in dialogue with others, being more used to instructional communication from parents and other adults.[12] Frequently this is seen as a result of modern lifestyles and adult attitudes towards children where the need to 'get things done' results in adults issuing instructions to children with the expectation that it will be followed, rather than taking the time to talk properly. Adults should be aware that the way they model communication will be copied and used by children; if we are good communicators children will tend to be so and vice versa.

Social play

This kind of play is similar to communication play in that it also challenges the accepted norms of society, whereby we are expected to follow the relevant rules and criteria for behaviour in certain situations. The play usually involves exaggerating social behaviour or subverting it, often with someone else as the 'butt' of the joke; usually a figure in authority. It uses similar skills to communication play such as irony, tone and body language, with the recognition of perceived or actual status among friends. In most groups there is a natural leader who has their jester or crony, the one who is allowed to make jokes at the leader's expense – but everyone knows who's really in charge. Hughes recognizes that social play has its 'darker side' and that to those observing, children given a subservient role may seem to be losing out.[13] But children need to know where they stand in the emerging social hierarchies if they are to survive in modern society. Social play is a way of finding out about the boundaries around 'good' or 'bad' behaviour, which will be seen as different in the varied environments and backgrounds children grow up in. That children by and large have limited status and so limited power has already been discussed, but social play is how they expose the lie of that belief, and show that most power can be deflated – when the giver stops 'playing the game', it is revealed for what it is.

Socio-dramatic play

When children are playing through real experiences in their lives (as contrasted with role play) they are engaged in socio-dramatic play. In this type of play, the drama is based on intense experiences of a social nature. Hughes states that, 'Socio-dramatic play is an important safety valve for children in highly charged social situations' such as difficult home circumstances, social bullying or simply falling-out with a friend.[14] By playing through the situations to their own outcomes, children are able to gain some level of emotional control on the real experiences; it's a way of rehearsing the feelings and actions without actual risk. Socio-dramatic play involves significant elements of openness and trust so children may play away from adult supervision in the quieter parts of a setting or private areas at home. When supporting children in socio-dramatic play, the need for adults to suspend judgement and encourage free expression is vital to the play form being satisfied – all children live very different lives and when they reveal themselves in this way, the adult's role is to support that emergence, rather than pass judgement on it.

By contrast Sara Smilansky, who worked with low-income migrant children in Israel, defined socio-dramatic play more generally as when two or more children cooperate in dramatic role playing. For Smilansky socio-dramatic play was an indicator of social and developmental competence, as she believed that children who lacked 'rich' cultural experiences had limited cognitive skills to succeed in other domains. Her practice suggested a low-intervention approach where adults aimed to preserve and enhance the socio-dramatic theme without changing its form. Smilansky created a four-step intervention programme where adults first provided a stimulus for play through visits or stories. Resources were then provided to support the anticipated play. Some children would engage with the materials, others would watch from the sidelines. After observation, the adult would then subtly intervene to bring those on the edge into the play. For example, a visit to a zoo might be supported back in a setting with costumes, masks and fake fur. Children might recreate the zoo with keepers and wild animals. The adult, noticing that one child was curious but not engaged, might take the role of an animal asking the keeper for some food. By asking if the curious child was also hungry, he might be brought into the play. The adult should then withdraw. Smilansky's research showed that this approach increased the children's incidence and involvedness with play, so leading to improved social and mental skills.

> **Key questions**
>
> There are two different approaches described for how to support socio-dramatic play with children; what do you think about them?
>
> - If you saw children playing in a dramatic and loud manner, would you intervene? What if they appeared to be cruel or violent (even if the violence was directed at a doll)?
> - Smilansky's approach has been criticized as being not applicable to all cultures and societies; some children use other forms of play such as role play to explore family issues. Observe children in their play, reflect and make up your opinion on this.
> - If you are in a play setting, how do the different approaches fit with the Playwork Principles?

As well as playing with their roles within groups, relationships and the social models in society, children are beginning to have a more direct influence on the world around them. The personal, political and economic powers of society impact on children both positively and negatively from the day they are born, with some forces affording children lots of choice in what they do and how they play and others very little. Some adults recognize that children have rights and responsibilities of their own and are able to get involved in the decisions about matters that affect them.

Participation – listening to children and young people

Pausing to listen to an airplane in the sky, stooping to watch a ladybird on a plant, sitting on a rock to watch the waves crash over the quayside – children have their own agendas and timescales. As they find out more about their world and their place in it; they work hard not to let adults hurry them. We need to hear their voices.

Cathy Nutbrown (1996)[15]

Not so long ago it was common in the UK to hear the phrase, 'Children should be seen and not heard.' In use since the fifteenth century (when interestingly it was first used specifically for young women), this proverb is now beginning to be challenged as emancipation begins to include children. In

1989 the United Nations Convention on the Rights of the Child was agreed for all children and young people under the age of 18. The Convention sets out 54 articles that detail children's rights under international law; all but 2 countries in the world have agreed to support the protocol. The Convention spells out the basic human rights that children and young people everywhere should have: the right to survival; to develop to the fullest; to protection from harmful influences, abuse and exploitation; and to participate fully in family, cultural and social life. A number of articles in the United Nations Convention relate to the right for children to have an active voice; these are Articles 12–17:

- Article 12 – When adults are making decisions that affect children, children have the right to say what they think should happen and have their opinions taken into account
- Article 13 – Children have the right to get and share information freely, as long as the information is not damaging to them or others
- Article 14 – Children have the right to think and believe what they want and to practice their religion
- Article 15 – Children have the right to meet together and to join groups and organizations
- Article 16 – Children have a right to privacy
- Article 17 – Children have the right to get information that is important to their health and well-being.

In summary, these articles give children the right to get information on matters that affect them, form their own opinions and say what they think is important, provided that they have respect for the rights and freedoms of others.

Since its adoption in the UK in 1991, and a subsequent inclusion of the rights into UK law, there has been a corresponding shift in society's approach to children. In 2005 the UK government appointed Professor Al Aynsley-Green as England's first Children's Commissioner, whose role was to 'give a voice' to all children and young people. Many local authorities and many voluntary sector organizations take into account children's opinions when making changes in services that affect them. All over the UK, there are projects that help children's voices be heard. A number of places have websites for children and young people to comment directly on issues, others use traditional newsletters. Some children's service teams have participation officers whose role is to work directly with children and young people supporting consultation work through a variety of methods.

Is children's participation necessary?

In the years since the United Nations Convention was adopted there has been a big shift in adults' attitudes towards children, but there is still a way to go. Some adults find it challenging to include children's opinions in decision making, arguing that children do not know what's best for them, especially if they are immature or have additional needs. Similar arguments were used in the past for excluding women, black people or disabled people from decisions that affected them. The issues involved are not easy to resolve; historically a lot of power has been invested in institutions (government, business, religion) that the majority of adults have little influence over, so why worry about children? Some commentators are concerned that involving children is tokenistic at best; adults control resources and spaces so they should be responsible for how they operate, passing that duty to children may be irresponsible. Others such as children's rights activist Roger Hart can point to instances of children's direct action changing the course of projects, especially in developing countries where social systems are in a state of flux.[16] Hart also comments on children who already make big decisions in their lives, children who care for others, children orphaned as result of adult disputes, and street children; it is not a question of whether children can make decisions, but how and in what circumstances.

The irony of course is that part of the value of play is that children are in control of play in the moment they are playing. Children on a playground can play, children in a bare room can play; they play in towns and in the country, indoors and out. Children don't need adult permission to play – they just do it. However the choices that adults make do have very significant impacts on children's opportunities to play. Adults' main role to help children play should be in the creation of spaces and opportunities so children and young people can engage with the world in as free a way as possible, with children choosing when to start or stop, and what to do in their play. Participation is an important development as it facilitates two characteristics that impact on children and young people. The first and most important is that it opens up the possibility for some adults that children might have something to say, that they are human beings in their own right – that is, it begins to change adults' attitudes towards children and young people. The second is that it involves adults in sharing some of the power and resources they hold; it introduces children and young people to the social and political structures under which they will live – and perhaps when they are adults they will more willingly engage with the systems, or have the skills to change them. We live in a world where economics, status and political power are valued; they may not be playful attributes but they have a big impact on children's play.

Participation methods

As the quote from Cathy Nutbrown above shows, all children have something to say about the world in which they live. Many guides have been written on how to consult with and include children and young people in the matters that affect their lives. These guides include a variety of tools for participation from adaptations of creative and playful activities, such as graffiti walls, collage making and model making, to variations on adult forms of involvement such as focus groups, consultation panels and meetings. Different tools may be adapted to suit varied ages, needs and abilities. Additional guides are now available that encourage contributions from children with disabilities, children unable to use speech or language to communicate and children for whom English is a second language. Judy Miller has written about how to include the voices of children as young as 3 and 4.[17]

Now that government policy requires children's settings to involve and consult with children, circle time and children's councils are active in many schools and settings. Circle time is a structured discussion technique, where everyone sits in a circle and has the opportunity to comment on the issue being discussed, or crucially not to comment if they so wish. It is seen as a democratic and open tool, though of course for children who are not used to speaking in public it may be intimidating. Children's councils echo the adult versions in that a representative of each class is elected to a central council that interacts with the staff in the school; they are often used in conjunction with circle times to help groups discuss issues at a local level before being raised in the council. As with all activities, these participation tools may be carried out in a tokenistic manner, going through the motions, or they may be used to help make change.

Adults' approaches to the task are important, as for instance, an involving process carried out in a patronizing or controlling way is missing the point. It's also vital that children are given feedback on what they have said; it's rarely possible to do everything that children ask for – they will come to understand this if clear explanations and follow-up information are given on the reasons why. And depending on their experience and confidence, children tend to focus on and comment about things that have happened recently in their lives. For instance, when asking children what they like about a setting, they may answer that they like the sandwiches, as the ones they had that day were good. The questioner may have wanted to know what they thought about the equipment or activities. When looking at improvements in play spaces, children tend to comment on what they have experienced, rather than what is possible, so that we often get a variation on the swing, slide and climbing frame provision. To help with this, we should offer children alternative experiences from which to make choices, by, for example, taking them to new settings with different types of environment and equipment. Once children have experienced a thing, it's easier for them to think about and comment on it. Children's participation is a contentious issue, but as with all emancipation processes, it starts by challenging attitudes before it begins to change behaviour; there is still a long way to go before we get it right.

Examples of changes in playful activity after listening to children

- The family usually went out together at the weekends, doing things that the parents wanted to do. After finding resistance from the children to some of the activities planned for the 'good of their health', the parents decide to change tack. They agreed that each family member would take it in turns to choose the activity they all did each Sunday. The mother decided on allotment work, the daughter going to the cinema, the son took them bowling and the father chose cycling. It worked – everyone knew that their turn would come and that if they didn't like it this week, they'd like it the next. The surprise was that they all enjoyed doing the lot – variety is the spice of life, even for grown-ups.

- The adventure playground needed rebuilding. Staff used a planning exercise to seek children's comments on ideas for playground changes. This work was promoted through a local magazine to encourage wider ownership and participation. Related work was generated through the use of a local 'graffiti' artist/graphic designer, who worked with children on a joint project. The results of the work were shown on site to parents and potential funders. The results were then written into a funding application for the site that was later successful in attracting substantial resources to develop the site in line with the children's original plans.

- The holiday playscheme was run by a dedicated staff team and student volunteers. Each year they would apply to the local council for aid to help provide play for local children. The grants came in varied amounts and some of it was not secured till the scheme was operating. To help share the resources around, the organizer split the scheme into ten different groups with lead staff in each group. After paying basic costs, the working budget would be split equally between the groups. The leaders offered the children a menu of activities ranging from visiting the zoo, the cinema, or go-karting to playing in the local park or even in the scheme building. When the children had made their choices the budget would be allocated to the choices. Invariably there would not be enough to go around so some negotiation was held to decide on what children really wanted to do. One trip to the zoo might be balanced with four trips to the local park; two trips swimming and three days in the building and so on. Every group would end up with something slightly different that their set of children had agreed upon.

Key questions

- Do you listen to children? If so, how and how often?
- What tools or methods do you use to get children's opinions?
- Have you used their ideas to help you decide on what to do?
- Did you give them feedback on what you could, and what you could not do?

Playing globally

Along with the increase in awareness of children's rights, there is a growing awareness of our connectedness to other human beings on the planet. The past 400 years has seen us as a species crossing and recrossing the world, making connections, taking from and sharing with others. In the last century, those connections have resulted in two world wars (and a 'cold war' and a 'war on terrorism'), a global market place of production and consumption and, mainly but not exclusively in the West, a 'Californication' of fashions and ideas. The past 20 years has seen an incredible growth in people making contact with people, first through cheap travel, then through the World Wide Web. Children today have never been more connected to, with knowledge of and involved with others across the globe. At a personal level, it is possible to speak to and play with others anywhere on the planet. Wi-Fi and the Net make it possible for children to sit in the garden with their laptop, talking to and interacting with others 5–10,000 miles away. The dangers of the internet are well known, but the opportunities to share ideas, feelings and thoughts are astonishing. Barriers are being removed and the old paradigms or power and belief are challenged. With the diversity of ideas and opinions open to us as a species, we might just have the ingenuity and resources to survive the changes ahead.

> We should always remember that, for we advanced mammals, the play moment begins in a tension between experiment and safety – the need to fully test out all the possibilities of being human, yet under conditions which are themselves not fatal, violent or beset with privation and pain. Is it too realistic to imagine an extended 'play moment' for our planet – where global sustainability and global creativity sustain and reinforce each other in a peaceful yet energetic spiral? If it is idealistic, then guilty as charged. Players are literally nothing if not congenital optimists. (Pat Kane 2004)[18]

'Playing with others' has explored how children can play with social and relationships concepts to understand their place in the world. In addition to the play types involved, we have looked at issues of personal and group power and how legislation is helping change adult attitudes towards children and young people.

'Playing with others' was the fourth quadrant of the Integral Play Framework, complementing active play, cultural play and play with thoughts and feelings. The four quadrants together help make clear how play is a phenomenon both of our minds and of our bodies, an experience that is 'within' and 'without' simultaneously. Balance in the quadrants and the types of play is satisfying and enjoyable in the moment but also good for the structure of our minds and our bodies, so helping us be healthy in all senses of the word. What we get from play is not specific knowledge but a knowingness about the world and ourselves. The Integral Play Framework helps us identify the qualities of each type of experience and what children (and adults) might get from those experiences. We may also see the factors that restrict and promote the freedoms for play in the interface of our personal world with the physical environment. When it's right, it feels right, being more than the sum of the parts, completing the play cycle and satisfying the drive that initiated the action to begin with. When does play end? We'll answer that in the next chapter, 'Grown-up play'.

Notes

1. Barrie Thorne adapted this phrase from Brian Sutton-Smith for her 1993 book *Gender Play – Girls and Boys in School* Buckingham: Open University Press p. 3.
2. Brian Eno (1994) *A year with swollen appendices* London: Faber and Faber p. 202.

3. This research on family play was based on Joe L Frost, Sue C Wortham and Stuart Reifel (2008) *Play and Child Development* by Upper Saddle River: Pearson Education Inc. pp. 208–209.

4. Professor Paul Gately is Carnegie Professor of Exercise and Obesity at Leeds Metropolitan University. He carries out research into childhood obesity treatment strategies.

5. Asbjørn Flemmen (2005) Real play: a recognized sensory-motor behaviour in Norway in *Playrights*, 26 (4) IPA.

6. *Play and Child Development* as quoted above pp. 216–217.

7. There is a good summary of the work of Slaughter and Dombrowski, who looked at gender and culturally specific play forms in *Play and Child Development* as quoted above pp. 203–206. Barrie Thorne's work (1993) *Gender Play* as quoted earlier also offers considerable insights into this subject.

8. Penny Holland (2003) *We Don't Play with Guns Here: War, Weapon and Superhero Play in the Early Years* Maidenhead: Open University Press.

9. Gregory Bateson (1973) *Steps to an Ecology of Mind* London: Granada Publishing.

10. Using words out of context, or malapropisms, was a frequent habit of Tommy Pickles of *The Rugrats* cartoon series produced by Nickelodeon, from which this example is taken.

11. This rhyme was adapted from David Rowan (21 May 2005) 'Have children really forgotten how to play?' *The Times Magazine* online.

12. BBC4 (6 June 2008) *A Revolution in Childhood*

13. Bob Hughes (2006) *Play Types – Speculations and Possibilities* London: London Centre for Playwork Education and Training p. 57.

14. Bob Hughes (2006) as quoted above p. 59.

15. Cathy Nutbrown (Ed.) (1996) *Respectful Educators – Capable Learners* London: Paul Chapman p. 53.

16. Roger Hart (1992) *Children's Participation: From Tokenism to Citizenship* Innocenti Essay 4, Florence: UNICEF International Child Development Centre.

17. Judy Miller (1997) *Never Too Young* London: National Early Years Network.

18. Pat Kane (2004) *The Play Ethic: A Manifesto for a Different Way of Living* London: Macmillan p. 21.

8 Grown-up play

When did you stop playing? 'Never.'

Rita (59 and a bit)

As up I grew, down I forgot.

ee cummings

Adventure is an adventure into the unknown. True play is without predetermined direction or definition. We are to explore, to learn as deeply as we can, to probe and experiment, and above all to laugh.

Brian Swimme (2001)[1]

Isn't it strange? Play is considered to be what children do, and when things are easy they are described as 'child's play'. Yet when we stop working, most people will do something that fits with the definition of play that a child gave us in Chapter 1: 'Play is what I do when everyone else has stopped

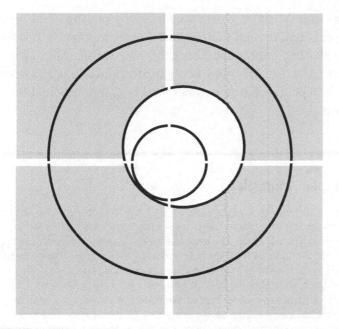

Figure 8.1 Grown-up play

telling me what to do.' Play for an adult satisfies the same drive as for children and in similar ways. The task for adults is to remain playful as they
grow older.

Key questions

Many adults stop 'playing' as they get older, nevertheless they still do things in their
spare time that are freely chosen and are not 'work'.

- Do you still play?
- How do you play?
- What do you do in your play?
- Who do you do it with?

Play satisfies many different needs, yet remains difficult to categorize
or give one label to. It moves between different activities, different moods
and different intensities, depending on the players, the environment and
the opportunities. Play themes can last for days but can also change in the

blink of an eye. When we grow up we may stop playing in the ways we did as young children, though there is lots of evidence that we still find it satisfying to play in all four quadrants either alone or in groups, with friends, testing our minds or our bodies, being creative and taking risks. Sometimes play may be repetitive but sometimes it takes us into new realities and new perspectives.

Example: Adult play

It was 10.30 a.m. when the two men in their twenties opened their first can of lager on the train to London. The two were heading to the Big City for some fun and were in a playful mood. The resources they had were themselves, 'Lads mags', mobile phones and cans of alcohol. The space they occupied was limited and defined by the table in front of the two seats where they sat.

Over the next 2 hours they read their magazines, shared comments, told jokes, told stories (some lewd) about mutual friends and family and drank another can of lager and two cans of cider. Behaviourally they consistently matched each other's movements and seating positions, were frequently bantering, occasionally gambling or playfighting. They had tremendous confidence in their own positions and when in the play frame were in their own private space. They frequently broke out of the frame, both by claiming other spaces physically and in terms of volume levels, and culturally as shown by the language and subject matter of their conversations – it was as if they were in a zone of privacy and confidentiality and were oblivious of others on the train.

As the example shows, adults' play may be very similar to children's or young people's play. We can identify physical play like rough and tumble, play with ideas and situations, play with roles, solitary play and group play. As with children's play there would have been times when bystanders felt that the activities were not appropriate for the space they occupied, but as described mostly the players were oblivious to those around them and not consciously setting out to upset others.

How adults play

Adults feel they tend to put away childish things as they take on the responsibilities of adulthood; it's probably fairer to say that our play changes when we grow up as research shows that adults engage in many types of play. Some grown-ups like mind games like crosswords and sudoku, others creative pastimes such as sewing or model-making; many join voluntary organizations to do similar things to what they do at work, but for fun, and some prefer to keep active in team or solitary sports. Brian Sutton-Smith has listed over 300 different play activities identified from both child and adult behaviours.[2] Here are a few examples, some of which may seem surprising:

- Gossip, riddles, stories, jokes, writing, going out after work, Saturday night fun, intimacy, playing on the internet, yoga
- Gambling, horoscopes, magical tricks
- Athletics, golf, card games, board games
- Hobbies, collections, birthdays, festivals, weddings, carnivals
- Dreams and daydreams, fantasies, ruminations, reveries
- Climbing, caving, orienteering, bungee jumping, mountain biking, long-distance running
- Playing tricks, playing around, playing on words, playing the fool.

As much as what is done, play is a mind-set; the way that you do an activity determines whether it is done playfully or otherwise: are you choosing to do it for yourself, are the goals set by yourself, do you find it satisfying (however you define that). We all have different personal definitions of what play is for and how we define play helps us see it in a certain way. Sutton-Smith has also categorized play definitions into seven different themes, the 'rhetorics', or self-evident beliefs; each is different to the other yet we understand the theme's connection to what we see in play behaviour.

- Play as Progress – play helps us growing and developing as human beings; exploring, mastering, learning through play, rehearsal for adulthood
- Play as Fate – chance or destiny controls all outcomes; games of chance, leaving all to circumstance, living in the moment
- Play as Power – exploring status and conflict; rule bound games, breaking the rules, playfighting, 'gamesmanship', *Games People Play*[3]
- Play as Identity – looking at identity and relationships; parades, festivals – whether religious or secular, sporting teams, cultural sports
- Play as the Imaginary – expressing flexibility and creativity; pretending, making believe, making art or music or drama, originality
- Play as Exploration of the Self – for the pleasure and satisfaction of the player; lost in play, play flow, just for the 'hell of it', ecstasy, higher states
- Play as Frivolous – a challenge to work and all that it represents; tricksters, jokers, anti-work, anti-system, playing the fool. (Sutton-Smith 1997 pp. 9–11)

Play is considered to be an activity that we do in our spare time, yet we spend a lot of time preparing for it and doing it. Think about the end of work on a Friday or Saturday; many people 'live' for this time off when they can let their hair down and go out with friends, dressed up, made up and looking forward to a good night out. An extension of this are the 'hen' and 'stag' nights organized for the bride and groom respectively prior to their wedding. These are frequently extremely playful rituals, well planned by the group supporting the event, with an element of surprise and embarrassment for the willing victim. Like all play, it may some times be taken too far, though generally these proceedings are accepted within the wider society as 'a bit of fun' and they pass off without serious incident.

Play for adults frequently has to be presented in an acceptable social context; the work ethic demands that having worked hard to earn our reward, we don't treat it too flippantly. A frame is set around the activities to delineate the play or leisure time from normal activity. To admit to talking playfully about sexual behaviour, or to parading in front of others in our underwear may be seen as inappropriate, but call it an 'Ann Summers' party and the expectations change.[4] Increasing numbers of people like to dress up and get into character for activities like theme parties or murder mysteries. The group bonding, social status, emotional release and fancy dress (shirts and scarves) are elements that make watching football such a successful pastime for many groups of people. Research papers have been written showing the benefits to mental health gained for fans in such areas as 'stress relief, catharsis and the development of good parent-child relationships'.[5]

Adults, as well as other types of play, also engage in 'deep play'; going through risky or potentially life-threatening experiences for the thrill of it. These include extreme sports such as going somewhere high and jumping off: bungee jumping, base jumping, hang gliding, paragliding, parachuting; testing yourself against the elements: wild camping, marathon running, ultra running, mountaineering, ice climbing, snow boarding; or simply going fast: street luge, down hill mountain-bike racing, motor bike racing, street racing, rallying, drag car racing, track racing, air plane racing and so on. Many of these activities, as well as being physically challenging, are also socially challenging in that they are out of the ordinary, sometimes illegal and tend to create a culture among participants who wear the badges of their activity with pride. The attraction of these activities is partly explained by the concept of *flow*.

Flow and intrinsic motivation

Mihaly Csikszentmihalyi ('Chicks send me high' as he playfully pronounces his name) is a researcher on positive psychology, looking at the nature of 'happiness'. While not writing expressly about play, his ideas have some accord with play processes. Csikszentmihalyi is best known for his work on the notion of *flow*, which is a state that occurs when a person is fully immersed in what they are doing. He says that flow is when the mind and the body are in a balanced state in order to accomplish a task. In his research, Csikszentmihalyi found that people reported being happiest at a task when being challenged and if the task was too easy or too hard the flow state would not occur; flow 'provided a sense of discovery, a creative feeling of transporting a person into a new reality...in short, it transformed the self by making it more complex'.[6] In the flow state, which has been described as an 'optimal state of intrinsic motivation', where people are doing things for their own reasons, they tell of the 'timelessness' of the moment, when all other considerations fall away and only the action is left. This feeling may occur in the middle of a tennis rally, while making a piece of music, narrating a story, running a race or climbing a mountain. Children in their play often seem to fall naturally into this state of timelessness; Csikszentmihalyi argues that as we grow older we need to rediscover happiness by seeking out 'optimal experiences' that help us find harmony and meaning in existence. As George Bernard Shaw put it, 'You don't stop playing as you grow old, you grow old because you stop playing.' Perhaps play serves higher functions than we recognize?

The value of play for adults

We [humans] had an intense curiosity that led us from our small tribal beginnings to conquer the whole surface of the planet in only a few thousand years – an amazing achievement for any animal species. The way we acquired this massively increased dose of curiosity was by becoming more childlike in our behaviour. It is an evolutionary process called neoteny and it sees a species retaining its infantile qualities into adult life. Where other primates abandon their juvenile playfulness as they become adult, we keep ours and develop it into sophisticated forms of 'adult play'. It is this adult play that has, over the centuries, given us all our greatest human achievements. Without it, we would be spending our time eating, mating, fighting, sleeping and cleaning ourselves. With it, we also have art, literature, music, theatre, sport, science and technology. (Desmond Morris 2005)[7]

For Desmond Morris, the drive to play has contributed to our discoveries in science and the arts. Edith Cobb put it this way: 'The ability to maintain plasticity of perception and thought is the gift of childhood to human personality' (1997 p. 35).[8] By staying childlike and retaining childlike playfulness, human beings have been able to continue exploring the world and our curiosity has led us into many areas both scientific and aesthetic. Throughout adulthood we retain the ability to expand our mental and physical awarenesses, until illness or old age set in. How we use that ability is up to the individual.

Just like children we may be unwilling to chance new ways of playing; as adults we have our comfort zones and don't like to move too far out of those. We might want for the confidence to try something different, or have a lack of knowledge based on limited experiences. As a consequence we can get 'stuck in a rut' doing things we've always done. There is a reassurance in doing things repetitively; we feel confident in our abilities and we feel 'understand' what we are doing; it helps keep us sane. However, if we are truly to be aware of our selves, we need to take risks to move beyond our current levels of operation, to transform our perceptions through new experiences. As much as I think I can walk across a tightrope I only know what it feels like after I've done it; till then my fear holds me back. If I want to tell a story to a group of children, the mistakes I might make hold me rigid until I take the step and do it; then I can look back and wonder what the fuss was all about.

Staying playful

Returning to the Integral Play Framework, adults will have reached various states of competence in each of the four quadrants; there is nothing to prevent us exploring further except our own preconceptions. This is especially valuable if we are to support children in their playing; to be playful, you need to play.

To maintain a playful mind we can keep the neurones firing with regular doses of humour. The ability to see the funny side of things helps keep our feet grounded but humour also helps the brain make new connections and stay creative and insightful. We should also exercise choice as much as possible, doing things we want to do, working through problems in our own way and at a speed that is comfortable where possible. This is easier said than done, but research shows that stress increases when people feel they have lost control over their lives. Seeking out new experiences and new challenges, whether mental or physical has benefits, as Csikszentmihalyi has shown. It is interesting that since the 1960s, many new forms of expression and self-discovery have arisen in the west as people seek those experiences that give their lives meaning, over and above the routine or work and existence.

Work is often about the fragmentation of tasks, compartmentalizing of processes; measuring/assessing/being objective, putting things in boxes (whether physically or metaphorically); it is specialist, frequently dispassionate and therefore suppressive or oppressive of individuality. And many feel that we have too much of those type of activities in the world. To counteract this, we need more play in the world; play that is involving, passionate, fun, satisfying, creative, stimulating, social, 'out of the box' and so challenging. In the 1980s the fitness boom took hold and people worked on their physical health and appearance; a corresponding search for 'inner fitness' has also arisen.

In many parts of the world, humans still celebrate local festivals, carnival and rituals; they seem to connect the people both physically and psychically to the places they live and the people in their community. Often in the West, these connections have been lost and we should address this in our lives through access to broad cultural activities including music, dance, art, theatre, games and stories. Traditional activities may be good for this, though for example just as effective are dance classes in salsa, ceroc or jive, where people come together socially through dance and rhythm. For people who like to dance in their own way, *5Rhythms* has grown in popularity in recent years. Founded by Gabrielle Roth, *5Rhythms* is a dance practice that uses recorded or live music to create different rhythms of dance to take people though five energy levels to arrive at a state of stillness or mediation. Ultimately the route taken to maintain or reconnect to these cultural activities is unimportant; what matters is making the effort.

As was discussed earlier in 'Playing actively', biophilia is the love of nature; people of all ages love to have access to the four elements (earth, air, fire and water) and opportunities to engage with nature or natural things. For some it may be gardening, for others it's allotment work, or walking or running the hills and valleys. Outdoor exercise is good for the body and the mind; it also helps humans keep up flexibility as they age. Maintaining balance and flexibility in all that we do is vital to help us keep a young attitude internally and externally.

When does play stop?

Perhaps the greatest test as we get older is to continue to seek out opportunities to do new things, to be playful, taking new risks to challenge our preconceptions (which may be pretty rigid). Those challenges will be different for all of us; with perhaps the biggest difficulty being to move towards the new risk, to take the first step. Playfulness is vital to our outlook on the world; doing things because they are the 'right thing to do' is not the same at all. 'Life is not a problem to be solved but a reality to be experienced.'[9] Being playful is always a continuing process, to which the answer to the question, 'Are we there yet?' is always, 'No'.

Looking back at the factors of play that were discussed in Chapter 3, these can be used to assess if an activity may be judged playful:

- Is it about 'now', with no concern for past for future outcomes?
- Does the activity fully engage the player?
- Is it a freely chosen activity?
- Can the player choose how to change or stop the activity?
- Is the activity challenging but not impossible?

Some of the things that adults do that may seem playful often lack some necessary ingredient: competitive sports, video games, luxury cruises and gambling on the stock market are not truly playful; they are mostly entertainment or recreation. Gwen Gordon describes this kind of activity as the 'near enemy' of play; something that resembles play but misses many of its vital qualities. She goes on:

> Neither is drug use, or shopping sprees. They are attempts to get relief from the grey backdrop of our play-deprived lives through forms of near-play that lack intimacy with the world. That is why near-play quickly becomes compulsive. It can never satisfy our deepest urges for true play.[10]

Many of these activities may be an acceptance of the current reality of the personal world, accepting things as they are. They become repetitive, boring, even addictive.

Playfulness helps to satisfy our curiosity about the world: what does this do, how does it connect to that? Why am I here, what is it all about? In true play, the play is continually creative and can carry on endlessly.

A 'beautiful intelligence'

Spiritually realized people tend to be the most mischievous, childlike, and playful of all.

Gwen Gordon (2003)

To say that play is essential to the human species is to corroborate what creative scientists, artists, and the great saints have understood as central to their own activities. Play, fantasy, the imagination, and free exploration of possibilities: these are the central powers of the human person. The development of the Earth depends on the development of the human into its destiny as the self-portrait of adventurous play.

Brian Swimme (2001 p. 123)

Play is the process by which humans make sense of the world around them, in a way that is meaningful for each individual. It is a flexible and adaptive process that can be described in many different ways that together can be understood as parts of a whole that holds and creates the human identity. This intelligence is what initially helps us survive in the world, then begin to understand it and eventually transcend it through our mind and spirit. Its beauty lies in the complexity of its seriousness and fun, in its protection and threat, in the conventional and the contradictory. This 'beautiful intelligence' is with us throughout life in every aspect of what it means to be human, some examples of which are given below. As we grow older, we choose (or are driven) to manifest our playfulness, our passion, our creativity in particular ways depending on our skills, beliefs and levels of confidence.

Play is not just a phenomenon for children; it is present throughout life and is there in the creativity and energy of many different kinds of people. In looking to the greatest minds, it is possible to find many examples of playfulness and playful approaches from every discipline of human activity.

An innate drive

In this first quote from one of the founding fathers of psychology, there are many connections to the playful process:

Art is a kind of innate drive that seizes a human being and makes him its instrument. The artist is not a person endowed with free will who seeks his own ends, but one who allows art to realize its purposes through him.

As a human being he may have moods and a will and personal aims, but as an artist he is 'man' in a higher sense – he is 'collective man' – one who carries and shapes the unconscious, psychic life of mankind. To perform this difficult office it is sometimes necessary for him to sacrifice happiness and everything that makes life worth living for the ordinary human being. (Carl Gustav Jung)[11]

The artistic drive that Jung spoke of is a cousin to the *ludido* or ludic drive[12] that 'seizes' all children when they play and 'lose their free will' in the playful moment; the process may start off as a conscious thought but becomes more when the conscious self merges with the unconscious to become free-flowing play. Jung suggests this is true for artists and alludes to the archetypes that flow through all artists to greater or lesser degrees. Through art (and play) we are connected to the human and universal past, while being very much present in the moment.

Edith Cobb told of the 'groundedness' of the playful engagement with the world, and how while it is related to the adult experience of art, it is not the same level of experience:

> The child's ecological sense of continuity with nature is not what is generally known as mystical. It is, I believe, basically aesthetic and infused with joy in the power to know and to be.[13]

The aim for adults should be to carry the sense of 'knowing and being' into their adult life, where it can enliven the everyday experience and also be enhanced by the adult sense of aesthetic awareness, seeing beauty in the world around them.

Rejected discoveries

Pablo Picasso, probably the most renowned artist of the twentieth century, commented on creativity:

> The picture is not thought-out and determined beforehand, rather while it is being made, it follows the mobility of thought...On each desecration of a beautiful find, the artist does not suppress it, to tell the truth; rather he transforms it, condenses it, makes it more substantial. The issue is the result of rejected discoveries...The artist is a receptacle of emotions from no matter where: from the sky, the earth, a piece of paper, a passing figure, a cobweb.[14]

Picasso describes how the art he produced was 'found' or 'received' from the environment and the unconscious. The process he describes as 'rejected discovery' takes place in every play setting where a child has a paintbrush in their hand; the art is the by-product or leftover from the process of creation. (Picasso is also an example of Jung's final point about artists making sacrifices for their art. Picasso was by no means a 'balanced' person and was a reported misogynist and bigot whose energies were directed towards his art.)

The process also has reference to the development of the individual's skills; 'how do I know that I can do a thing until I try?' The child tries an activity then looks at what the experience does for them and amends or works with that product. In this way, the child makes the discovery that what was unknown is now known, or what was once difficult is now easy. This occurs at all stages of life, but is most obvious in the growing child.

Combinatory play

On the matter of skill developments being combined to produce new concepts, Albert Einstein said that he often felt or experienced the concept before he was able to verbalize it in language:

> The words or the language, as they are written or spoken, do not seem to play any role in my mechanism of thought. The psychical entities which seem to serve as elements in thought are certain signs and more or less clear images which can be 'voluntarily' reproduced and combined. There is, of course, a certain connection between those elements and relevant logical concepts. It is also clear that the desire to arrive finally at logically connected concepts is the emotional basis of this rather vague play with the above mentioned elements. But taken from a psychological viewpoint, this combinatory play seems to be the essential feature in productive thought – before there is any connection with logical construction in words or other kinds of signs which can be communicated to others.[15]

The originator of the Theory of Relativity stated that he needed to play in order to think productively – and that that play *preceded* the symbolic formulas that he then used to communicate the thought to others.

A terrific ecstasy

A more emotional description is given by the writer and philosopher Nietzsche to show how he responded to or found his new thoughts:

> The notion of revelation describes the condition quite simply; by which I mean that something becomes visible and audible with indescribable definiteness and exactness. One hears – one does not seek; one takes – one does not ask who gives: a thought flashes like lightning; inevitably without hesitation – I have never had any choice about it. There is an ecstasy whose terrific tension is sometimes released by a flood of tears; during which one's progress varies from involuntary impetuosity to involuntary slowness. There is the feeling that one is utterly out of hand...When my creative energy flowed most freely; my muscular activity was always greatest. The body is inspired.[16]

Nietzsche also comments here on two other experiences that are shared with the playful process. The first is 'the feeling that one is utterly out of hand', similar to when a child is in play flow and *anything* can happen. And the related experience, which shows the connection between body and mind; 'when *I* feel good, my *body* feels good also'.

Auto-erotism

So far, we have heard about the positive experiences of the creative, playful process. But of course, play may not always be positive from an observer's point of view. Jung has already commented that artist can sacrifice happiness in order to respond to the creative drive, here he goes further:

> the creative force can drain the human impulses to such a degree that the personal ego must develop all sorts of bad qualities – ruthlessness, selfishness and vanity (so-called 'auto-erotism') – and even every kind of vice, in order to maintain the spark of life and to keep itself from being wholly bereft.

Jung goes on, with a direct reference to a similar effect in children:

> The auto-erotism of artists resembles that of... neglected children who from their tenderest years must protect themselves from the destructive influence of people who have no love to give them – who develop bad qualities for that very purpose and later maintain an invincible egocentrism by remaining all their lives infantile and helpless or by actively offending against the moral code or the law.[17]

With reference to the Integral Play Framework, we can interpret this statement as being a child who has a poorly developed sense of identity, may also have a poorly developed sense of culture or society – 'the moral code or the law'. Certainly we can see the connection between deprivations in the earliest years affecting children throughout their lives; the children have no choice but to protect themselves from the hostile environment that they find themselves in.

Daemon or demon

The potential for experiences to shape us for good or ill is revealed in this quote from *Grace and Grit* by Ken Wilber. The book is about the last five years of Treya Wilber's life after she was diagnosed with a virulent cancer. As do many people faced with death, Treya asked herself what she wanted to do with the time left to her; Wilber explains it as follows:

> This was by no means the solution or the final version of Treya's search for her vocation, for her 'true work,' but it was a start. I could sense a shift in her, an

inner healing of sorts, an integrating, a balancing. We came to refer to her search for her 'work' as a search for her 'daemon' – the Greek word that in classical mythology refers to 'god within', one's inner deity or guiding spirit, also known as a genii or jinn, the tutelary deity or genius of a person; one's daemon or genii is also said to be synonymous with one's fate or fortune. Treya had not yet found her fate, her genius, her destiny, her daemon, not in its final form, anyway . . . Her daemon, really, was her own higher Self, and it would soon be expressed, not in work, but in art.

Wilber says that looking within to what is best within us, is a way of connecting to a higher Self, or being true to ourselves and what we are capable of. He continues:

But there is a strange and horrible thing about one's daemon: When honoured and acted upon, it is indeed one's guiding spirit; those who bear a god within bring genius to their work. When, however, one's daemon is heard but unheeded, it is said that the daemon becomes a demon, or evil spirit – divine energy and talent degenerates into self-destructive activity. The Christian mystics, for example, say that the flames of Hell are but God's love denied, angels reduced to demons.[18]

So not being true to ourselves, by not heeding the true spirit, we are in danger of becoming self-destructive. Whether we believe in a higher self or not, this example speaks of the opportunities we have within ourselves and the potential for growth we carry. The outcomes are determined in part by what we chose to engage with in life; are we confident enough to risk a little in order to learn a lot? Or do we remain 'stuck' at a level of development, forever wondering why the grass is greener for others? The pain of failure is somehow less than the pain of regret.

A metaphysical hue

The journey through life is given a metaphysical hue by the writer Henry James. James speaks of a friend who 'deludes' himself (from the Latin *deludere* 'to play falsely') about the point of a creative act. James was commenting on writing but likened the experience to life itself:

Knut Hamsun once said, in response to a questionnaire, that he wrote to kill time. I think that even if he were sincere in stating it thus he was deluding himself. Writing, like life itself, is a voyage of discovery. The adventure is a metaphysical one: it is a way of approaching life indirectly, of acquiring a total rather than a partial view of the universe. The writer lives between the upper and lower worlds: he takes the path in order eventually to become that path himself.

> I began in absolute chaos and darkness, in a bog or swamp of ideas and emotions and experiences. Even now I do not consider myself a writer, in the ordinary sense of the word. I am a man telling the story of his life, a process which appears more and more inexhaustible as I go on. Like the world-evolution, it is endless…It is this quality about all art which gives it a metaphysical hue, which lifts it out of time and space and centres or integrates it to the whole cosmic process.[19]

James makes a direct connection to the creative person living between the 'upper and lower worlds' – which could be seen as the unconscious and conscious or the conscious and supraconscious worlds. He goes on to say that life becomes the journey and that it is the 'telling itself' that becomes the goal. What is clear in James' writing is that his experiences take him from darkness and raise him up into an evolutionary state that goes on through life – which he states is 'endless' and connected to the whole cosmos.

A playful intelligence

We can now see that, as explained by the Integral Play Framework and as experienced by many people in many different disciplines, the playful process is active at the interface:

- between the object and the subject
- between feelings and facts
- between 'me' and the world
- between 'me' and 'us'.

Play is an intelligence that helps us understand and so shape our world to serve our needs. It may be seen as the most human of characteristics in that it lifts us, stage by stage, from the animal world into the world of thought and spirit. Edith Cobb in her book *The Ecology of Imagination in Childhood* has many things to say about this playful experience and how it shapes the child, level by level:

> Self-knowledge and a sense of identity are achieved only by means of interplay between the organism and its total environment and that all 'knowing' emerges progressively at each level of organisation.[20]

Cobb stresses the importance of this interplay and how it begins with the physical world then rises to become the most human of actions:

> In actuality we cannot know anything about ourselves or the world without making comparisons with forms other than the self. This comparison begins at

the level of immediate perception and proceeds into the realm of thought and ideas.[21]

The thinking here is in accord with that of Wilber and the Integral Play Framework; the child's subjective reality is shaped and influenced by interaction with the objective world. The child's connection to both worlds starts off at the most basic and then develops to the conscious and higher conscious levels.

So in summary, and drawing upon the comments of the many people quoted, it can be said that we exist in the world at the interface of the *personal ecology* (feelings, symbols, thoughts, concepts) and the *physical ecology* (environment and others). The quality of both ecologies affects that experience; 'I cannot exist without the world, and the world is created (for me) by my experience of it.'

Edith Cobb comments on this consciousness within the child and in so doing connects the process in the individual to the whole of creation:

> The child's urge to 'body forth the forms of things unknown' in the microcosm of child art and play bears a distinct resemblance to the morphogenesis [form making] characteristic of nature's long-term history, namely, evolution.[22]

Figure 8.2 Don't stop playing!

This playful consciousness[23] is the beautiful intelligence that guides us through this experience, opening up worlds of possibility and wonder at every step.

The value of play – keep playing

So now get playing… ideally with some children that you know, but if not then with your parents, friends, neighbours, even workmates! And remember:

> The opposite of play… is not work… it is depression. (Brian Sutton-Smith)[24]

Notes

1. Brian Swimme (2001) *The Universe is a Green Dragon* Rochester: Bear and Co. p. 122.
2. Brian Sutton-Smith (1997) *The Ambiguity of Play* London: Harvard University Press pp. 4–5.
3. *Games People Play* (1964) is a book by Eric Berne, using Transactional Analysis to describe how people interact through the social scenarios we play out in our day-to-day relationships with people.
4. *Ann Summers* is a chain of UK high street shops selling raunchy underwear and sex toys.
5. Alan Pringle (2004) 'Can watching football be a component of developing a state of mental health for men?' *The Journal of the Royal Society for the Promotion of Health*, 124 (3), 122–128.
6. Mihaly Csikszentmihalyi (1990) *Flow – The Psychology of Optimal Experience* New York: Harper and Row p. 74.
7. Taken from *Bailey's Democracy* (2005) London: Thames and Hudson for which Desmond Morris wrote the introduction, no page numbers given.
8. Edith Cobb (1977) *The Ecology of Imagination in Childhood*, Dallas: Spring Publications p. 35.
9. Søren Kierkegaard in Laurence Peter (1977) *Quotations for Our Time* London: Souvenir Press p. 303.
10. Gwen Gordon (2003) 'Play: the movement of love' *EarthLight Magazine* No48, 13 (3). Accessed from www.earthlight.org/2003/essay48_gordon.html
11. Carl Gustav Jung quoted in Brewster Ghiselin (1952) *The Creative Process* Berkeley: University of California Press p. 229.
12. The ludido was described by Gordon Sturrock in Sturrock and Else (1998) 'The playground as therapeutic space: playwork as healing' – aso known as 'The Colorado Paper', in *Therapeutic Playwork Reader One* (2005) Southampton: Common threads p. 81.
13. Edith Cobb (1977) as quoted above pp. 15–16.
14. Pablo Picasso quoted in conversation reported by Christian Zervos, in Ghiselin (1952) *The Creative Process* as quoted above pp. 49–51.
15. Letter to Jacques Hadamard, in Ghiselin (1952) *The Creative Process* as quoted above p. 32.
16. Composition of *Thus Spoke Zarathustra*, Friedrich Nietzsche, in Ghiselin (1952) *The Creative Process* as quoted above pp. 209–210.

17. Carl Gustav Jung, in Ghiselin (1952) *The Creative Process* as quoted earlier p. 230.

18. Ken Wilber (1991) *Grace and Grit* Dublin: Newleaf p. 58.

19. Henry Miller: Reflections on Writing, in Ghiselin (1952) *The Creative Process*, as quoted earlier p. 184.

20. Edith Cobb (1977) as quoted earlier p. 56.

21. Edith Cobb (1977) as quoted earlier p. 53.

22. Edith Cobb (1977) as quoted earlier pp. 15–16.

23. Gordon Sturrock named this a *ludic consciousness* in Sturrock and Else (1998) as quoted earlier p. 84.

24. Brian Sutton-Smith (1997) as quoted earlier p. 198.

9 A play history – From Plato to the play ethic

You can discover more about a person in an hour of play than in a year of conversation.

Plato (427–347 BCE)

Play will be to the 21st century what work was to the last three hundred years of industrial society – our dominant way of knowing, doing and creating value.

Pat Kane (1964–)

Like the practice of play, play theory has evolved, yet the key elements have remained fundamentally the same over the past 2,000 years; much of what we now say about play would still be recognized by the early Greeks and Romans.[1] Many of the writers and thinkers in this list would normally be recognized for their contributions in fields other than play, yet all have something to say about play and its value.

The Greeks with their interest in athleticism and physical prowess recognized the need for a 'healthy mind in a healthy body'.[2] The Greek philosopher **Plato** advised teaching solely through festivals, games, songs and amusements. In his essay, *The Republic*, Plato agreed with **Aristotle** that children's play was directed towards their education – intellectual, practical and moral. Aristotle thought that children's games anticipated the jobs that children would have later in life as adults and parents; during play, they would practice the skills necessary to be capable humans. Plato also wrote about what we now call the physiological benefits of play – how play is good for our bodies. He said that children needed to run and jump in their play, using their bodies to develop their muscles and balancing abilities; athletics were highly prized by the Greeks (though only for 'citizens' and not for women or slaves).

After the Romans, the European countries entered the so-called Dark Ages from which time little is known of the lives of children and their play. We can see from the stories surviving from that time that while play was permitted for children of the ruling clans, for most childhood was a time of preparation for adulthood; 'playtime' and what we now call leisure was fitted in around duties. It was in the seventeenth century that **John Locke** (1632–1704) recognized that toys could be used to help children learn through play. He recommended that children create their own playthings from the simple everyday objects they found in their environment. Locke also argued for the use of educational toys such as dice and alphabet blocks. However, Locke did not value play for its own sake, believing that children's play should be directed towards what he considered to be 'good and useful habits'.

In the eighteenth century, the philosopher **Jean Jacques Rousseau** (1712–1778) stressed the importance of play, experimentation and freedom in education and development. Rousseau believed children learn from their surroundings and from first-hand experiences through trial and error. To this end, he recognized how important it was for children to have some experience of challenge in their environment. This emphasis on learning by doing was supported by **Johan Pestalozzi** (1746–1827). He held that children are innately good and that it is society that corrupts them.

Friedrich Schiller (1759–1805) commented[3] on the 'surplus energy' theory of play, which said that when animals had no need to find food or defend themselves from predators, they spent energy in 'aimless activity'. While focusing on the physical energy needed for play, Schiller also wrote about what he called the 'play impulse' in humans. He saw this impulse as a 'free' activity (not work related) that helped humans develop beyond their basic animal nature to that of rational human beings. He recognized that this activity was intrinsic – it emerged from within the individual.

In 1840, **Friedrich Froebel** (1782–1852) created the word *kindergarten* – young children's garden – to describe the Play and Activity Institute he had founded in Germany. Froebel highlighted the importance of the child's free play as a contribution to their learning and development. Activities in the first kindergarten included singing, dancing, gardening and playing with the *Froebel Gifts*, simple wooden shapes that were intended to provide material for children's self-directed activity.

Written in the middle of the nineteenth century, Charles Darwin's theory of evolution focused attention on the biological and physiological aspects of play. Different aspects of the implications of this theory were picked up by various writers. **Herbert Spencer** (1820–1903) writing in his autobiography[4] updated Schiller's 'surplus energy' theory and argued that because parents provided for their young, children had energy to use for play; he described play as 'an artificial exercise of powers' caused by the lack of natural release through 'real actions' such as chasing or competition. **Granville Stanley Hall** (1846–1924) is known for his recapitulation theory of development. This was based on the principle that growing children would repeat – recapitulate – evolutionary stages of development as they grew up. Hall felt there was an association between evolutionary history and the stages of childhood and that every child had a capacity to attain knowledge in the same order.

Karl Groos (1861–1946) wrote that play must be evolutionary as it was the more advanced species that played more and for longer periods. He felt that play gave children the ability to use skills in many different conditions. Groos argued that play was a method through which children made sense of adult roles within society and that play was therefore preparation for adulthood.

Sigmund Freud (1856–1939) was concerned with the relationship between imaginative play and emotion. He believed play was crucial in order to repeat, or 'play through' a traumatic event that enabled children to overcome that trauma and gain mastery over the event. He recognized that the child may be influenced by their own unconscious and conscious desires and needs, which while influenced by the world around them were independent of it.

Around the end of the nineteenth century, many writers became interested in the role of play in education. **Rudolf Steiner** (1861–1925) said that education should aim to help children fulfil their own potential mentally, physically and emotionally. He encouraged children to focus on play, drawing and storytelling until the age of 7. Steiner said that children should be respected as individuals, who should be encouraged to learn at their own pace, and not as needed by others.

John Dewey (1859–1952) also strongly believed that education should be 'child centred' and active – children should learn and use skills that helped fulfil their potential as human beings. He believed in 'learning by doing' and taught children about the formal subjects by exploring the methods of everyday activities such as cooking. However Dewey felt the role of the teacher was crucial in helping children make sense of their world on the basis of the teacher's greater knowledge and understanding.

Maria Montessori (1870–1952) said all activities were meaningful for children; she did not differentiate between work and play. She believed children learn by using their senses and that they learn everything from their surroundings; she stressed that creating a stimulating, interesting environment was as critical as what the adult did with the children. She was the first educator to develop child-size furniture and real equipment for children to use.

Montessori wanted children to be responsible for their own learning with the adult in support of the children's learning and considered it the high indicator of success when the adult was able to withdraw to let children play and learn by themselves.

The founder of analytical psychology was **Carl Gustav Jung** (1875–1961), who worked closely with Freud for a time but then broke away with his own ideas about the *psyche*, 'the totality of all psychic processes, conscious as well as unconscious'. Jung had widely travelled and studied both Eastern and Western philosophy before coming to his conclusion that balance and harmony were necessary for human well-being. He recognized the role that the play drive had in relation to creativity and said that the reason behind play and creativity was not fully conscious and was often affected by deeper, more unconscious influences.

> The creation of something new is not accomplished by the intellect, but by the play-instinct acting from inner necessity. The creative mind plays with the object it loves. (CG Jung 1981)[5]

Like Jung, **Johan Huizinga** (1872–1945) studied Eastern philosophies and was fascinated by the role of the jester in Indian tales; the character of the fool who by playing is able to break all the rules and make fun of those in charge. In 1938 Huizinga wrote *Homo Ludens* – 'Playing Man' – in which he wrote about the importance of the play element of culture and society; he was one of the first writers to recognize that play was valuable of itself. Huizinga suggested that play was the foundation of all the key forces of culture and society: law and order, commerce and profit, craft and art, poetry, wisdom and science.

> Play is a uniquely adaptive act…with a special function of its own in human experience. (Huizinga 1938)[6]

Jean Piaget (1896–1980) was a developmental psychologist whose ideas have been very influential on late twentieth-century teaching. His key thought was that children constructed their own knowledge by giving meaning to the people and things in the world around them in order to build a model of that world in their minds. Piaget considered play as a means towards development during which children repeated what they were familiar with. He is best known for his 'ages and stages' theory of cognitive development. Piaget believed that children pass through four clear stages where they (1) learn through the senses, (2) begin to form generalized thoughts, then (3) create ideas based on reasons from their perspective through to (4) thinking conceptually. This model is still the dominant approach in Western education even though we know that the stages are a general description rather than an accurate map; it is recognized individual children will develop in different ways according to their own experience and desire.

Lev Vygotsky (1896–1934) was active at the same time as Piaget, Freud and Montessori, though his influence only developed later in the twentieth century when the approach of children's workers in Reggio Emilia, Italy (see below) was shared with the wider world. Vygotsky was influential in that he considered the (subjective) observation of children's abilities as valid as the achievements they made based on (objective) measurements of development. He showed that social and cognitive developments were not separate and that the one supported the other – and that children were able to learn from their peers as well as adults. He recognized that children's lives were influenced by their families, communities and the wider world. He believed that communication and interaction were vital to children's construction of knowledge on many levels; adults or other children help individuals reach a new skill or awareness by giving appropriate support as the individuals try out new approaches or new situations.

> In play a child always behaves beyond [their] average age, above [their] daily behaviour. In play it is as though [they] were a head taller than [themselves]. (Lev Vygotsky 1978)[7]

Donald Woods Winnicott (1896–1971) was a playful individual who is best remembered for contributing some key concepts to the study of children's well-being. Winnicott, while building on Freud's work, was a psychoanalyst quite independent in his thinking. He felt that the relationship between the infant and their environment was key to healthy development and that the strongest and most enduring relationship was between the child and their primary carer – usually the mother. Observing how carers would change and develop their responses to children as they grew, he referred to the primary carer as the 'good enough mother' – that is, from the child's point of view, mothers are never seen as 'perfect' so 'allowing' the child to sort out their own way to grow up. Winnicott saw that children relate to things as 'mine' and 'not mine' – he termed these 'me' and 'not-me' or 'other'. He felt that this differentiation of the self and the other was crucial to healthy development. He wrote much about this change and the positive and negative effects of it. For example, he felt the 'true self' would emerge after a healthy separation from the carer and the 'false self' may develop as a protection mechanism if the child felt threatened or insecure by the separation.

Recognizing how the soft toys and blankets that most children carry with them in their early years are comforters for an absent carer, Winnicott created the term 'transitional object' to describe these comforters. The transition referred to was as the child changed from dependence on the carer to independence. Key to helping the child become independent was the creation by the carer of the 'holding environment' – a space where the child, while still in the care of the adult, is able to act by themselves. The holding environment is considered to be both physical and psychic as it is based on trust between the parent and child; the space should be large enough to allow independent movement and small enough to offer reassurance by way of a smile or gentle support. The size of the space will vary according the child's confidence and ability. In his work, Winnicott emphasized the need for empathy, humour and creativity and was a playful person himself, well liked by those he worked with.

After studying with Anna Freud (whose work was influential in the development of play therapy), **Erik Erikson** (1902–1994) developed his theory of psychosocial development and his Eight Stages of human development. Erikson gave us the term 'identity crisis' and he considered it unavoidable that children and young people experience crisis as they grow towards adulthood. He felt it vital that children develop trust in the people around them and that they learn to act independently, using their own initiative in order to become competent. Erikson stressed that it was important to give children simple choices so that they learn to make their own decisions. He also considered it essential that adults were 'honest' and authentic in their relationships with children, even if children displayed wild changes of ability and mood as they grew. Erikson knew that it was necessary to focus on the positive changes rather than the mistakes made along the way.

> The playing adult steps sideward into another reality; the playing child advances forward to new stages of mastery. (Erik Erikson 1977)[8]

Carl Rogers (1902–1987) was known for his development of person-centred psychology. He did not write expressly about play or playwork, though his ideas on what it is to be human have crossed into many other disciplines. In his work, Rogers[9] described what he called 'The Fully Functioning Person'; the characteristics of whom could be descriptive of the playing child. Such a person according to Rogers lived life to the full, would be creative, open to new experiences, able to trust their own judgement, and able to make a wide range of choices. Other characteristics are that the person would live a 'rich' life, coping with a range of emotions from high to low and would be trusted by others as someone who could act constructively. Rogers also spoke about the need for people to live 'authentic' lives as far as they were able, arguing that many people did not fully achieve their potential due to the constraints they accepted in order to conform to other's expectations. Rogers felt that by 'launching oneself fully into the stream of life', we are able to truly become ourselves and fully functioning on all levels.

Jerome Bruner (1915–), an American psychologist, built on the work of both Piaget and Vygotsky to write about children's learning in 1966.[10] Bruner proposed that children (and adults) learn best by doing something themselves, then seeing a visual representation of that act and then they may understand the language describing the act. In contrast to Piaget, Bruner understood that these elements support one another and do not fit into clearly defined stages; children will behave differently from each other. For Bruner, play was important for trying out new actions or new combinations of actions in less risky situations. Developing Vygotsky's work, Bruner saw the role of the adult in supporting children was to 'scaffold' new opportunities and experiences by providing resources and guidance if necessary, though his intent was for the child to do things for themselves.

> The main characteristic of play – child or adult – is not its content, but its mode. Play is an approach to action, not a form of activity. (Jerome Bruner)[11]

Working in 1968, **Sara Smilansky** studied children at play in Israel and the USA. Through her work, she came to the conclusion that what she termed culturally disadvantaged children did not know how to play imaginatively and that this was a serious hindrance to their ability to read and write. She felt that the cultural world surrounding the child was important to their overall development. Smilansky stated that dramatic and socio-dramatic play were an important means of children developing mental, social and emotional skills. She defined dramatic play as the play of children when they pretend to be someone else and socio-dramatic play as when two or more children cooperate in dramatic role playing.

Desmond Morris (1928–), famous for his book *The Naked Ape* suggested that play behaviour in humans is a distinct and separate drive. He believed this drive was to provide humans with a subtle and complex awareness of the world and their abilities in relation to it. He observed that children in their play investigate the unfamiliar until it becomes known, playing with things in as many ways as possible, selecting the most satisfying at the expense of the others, combining and recombining these variations, one with another for their own sake. Morris considered that humans needed as wide a range of experiences as possible to help them solve the problems that the world presents – in order to be successful as adults, children must be 'super-active' and their natural playfulness encourages that level of activity.

> We often contrast 'play' behaviour with 'serious' behaviour, but perhaps the truth is that we would be better off treating play as the most serious aspect of all our activities. (Desmond Morris 1977)[12]

In 1977, **Catherine Garvey** wrote the influential book *Play*. While written for 'educators', Garvey also wanted to explain to parents and other adults about the phenomenon of play. She therefore writes from biological and developmental perspectives as well as for educational environments. The book starts with a chapter called 'What is Play?' and after reviewing some of the key theories, sets out an inventory of the characteristics of play, some of which are recognizable from the current UK nationally accepted definition quoted in Chapter 1:

- Play is pleasurable, enjoyable
- Play has no extrinsic goals
- Play is spontaneous and voluntary
- Play involves some active engagement on the part of the player
- Play has certain systematic relations to what is not play.[13]

Garvey also recognized with the last point that play behaviour is not limited to just one field but had links with 'creativity, problem solving, language learning, the development of social roles, and a number of other cognitive and social phenomena'. She explained – in contrast to some of other theorists quoted above – that play should be seen as more than a particular set of actions; Garvey considered it to have 'no particular behaviour or objective unique to itself', feeling that play patterns were 'borrowed' from other human actions. For example, children can play with the concepts of fright, flight and fight, and with language, art and relationships. In particular, she broke away from Piaget's ideas of cognitive development by showing how play has separate lines of development in other areas, for example, communication, motion, rules and rituals. Garvey stressed that play has primarily a strong social dimension; it is about playing with others as well as playing for oneself. In the conclusion to her research, she stated that it was 'difficult, if not impossible, to propose any single or uniform function for play', feeling that play was possible with different resources at different age levels for different benefits. Garvey ended with a strong plea for adults to observe children at their play as she felt we have much to learn from simply letting them play.

In 1964, **Loris Malaguzzi** (1920–1994) founded a network of early childhood centres in Reggio Emilia, a town in northern Italy. The *Reggio Approach* – which includes community and parental support, the use of the physical environment, seeing adults as learners, and the exploration of drawing, sculpture, dramatic play and writing; what Malaguzzi called the different 'languages' of children – is now admired worldwide. He believed that schools should be made fit for children, who he said can think and act for themselves and who are 'active constructors' in their own learning. Malaguzzi's philosophy, 'one that recognizes the rights of children and the obligations of humanity', has impacted on the Reggio Emilia network so that children continue to be supported to develop their own themes and to explore their whole world: mind and body, emotions and thoughts. The Reggio Approach is now being adopted and promoted throughout the UK and elsewhere across the world.

The author of over 50 books on play, **Brian Sutton-Smith** (1924–) has researched play in many forms. Originally a psychologist, he has extended his studies into play history, folklore and education. He does not consider that play is purely a childhood phenomenon and in his book *The Ambiguity of Play* (1997) he has listed over 300 different forms of play as exhibited in both child and adult behaviours. Examples of these include: dreams, daydreams, ruminations and reveries; hobbies, collections, flower arranging, using computers; playing tricks, playing around, playing for time and so on. In his work[14] Sutton-Smith defines play both biologically and psychologically; saying that the first function of play is to reinforce the organism's behavioural variability from the actual to the possible – from what we can do to what we might do. The second psychological function is 'as a lifelong stimulation' for newness and new forms of experience, which he sees as essential for ensuring that we persevere through the trials that life has to offer – whether those trials are sought out (as in personal challenges) or freely arising (as when problems emerge in the environment or in personal relationships). Sutton-Smith is an advocate for children making their own decisions in their play; he points out that as adults we often 'forget' that our own beliefs and expectations can get in the way of children playing – we can see how other people are intruding into children's play but our own well-meaning intensions we cannot see, particularly if we are working with very young children.

> Either child's play is their area of freedom as adult recreation is our area of freedom, or we are treating the children as a lower caste, idealizing play while we manipulate it to fit our preconceived purposes. (Brian Sutton-Smith 1988 p. 4)[15]

Gordon Burghardt (1941–) is one of the leading animal behaviourists of recent times. He is interested in the evolution and development of play, which he labels 'surplus resource theory'[16] – an echo of the work of Schiller, Spencer and Hall. In his book *The Genesis of Animal Play*, he shows that as well as humans and mammals, other animals including fish and reptiles will play. He explores the role that play has in our understanding of evolution, the brain, behaviour and psychology. He proposes that playfulness may have been essential to the origin of much that we consider distinctive in human (and mammalian) behaviour; he has described the process of play as an 'evolutionary pump' that helps develop new cognitive abilities and social behaviours. He ranks these processes in a threefold hierarchy: primary – play that is not related to any outcomes; secondary – play that is necessary to maintain physiological states; and tertiary – play that helps the animal gain a new role or skill. Burghardt also recognizes that all play behaviour will be affected by a number of factors including levels of energy in the animal, surplus resources to play with, levels of parental care and heritable variations in play behaviour and the environmental context – that is, the opportunity to play.

In 1982, **Bob Hughes** (1944–) started what became a series of meetings as part of *Play Education*, 'an alternative way of learning about what play has to offer us'. Since then Hughes has worked with and had an influence on many people working in the play sector in the UK. In addition to the platform created by Play Education, he was also the founder and editor of the *International Play Journal* that ran from 1993–1996. Hughes started his playwork career at Puddlebrook Adventure Playground in Haverhill in 1970 after initially training as a teacher. He wrote his first paper 'Notes for Adventure Playworkers' in 1975, and since then has written numerous articles and several books that have influenced the way that playworkers support children in their play. Throughout his career in playwork, Hughes has maintained a contact with playing children, often working with children on sites as well as writing about play and contributing to influential documents that have affected adult practice. From the earliest papers is the consistent belief that supporting children to find their own solutions for coping with a 'hostile world' is at the heart of best practice. In his largest text to date, *Evolutionary Playwork and Reflective Analytic Practice* (2001), Hughes argues that adult-free play is essential for the psychological well-being of the child. He recognizes the challenges that this perspective causes to the dominant view in the UK, but Hughes has always been a passionate advocate for children's play and unapologetically declares that this freedom can result in actions that may be seen as socially unacceptable but are nevertheless fundamentally important to the child. Hughes was recognized in 2008 for his contribution to the field with the award 'Lifetime in Play' from London Play.

One of the speakers at the first Play Education Meeting, **Frank King** (1950?–1989) had a short but influential career in playwork. King worked on a variety of adventure playgrounds from 1972 and later for the National Playing Fields Association and Bristol City Council. In 1988 King wrote the paper *The Right to Play* that was part of the Play Policy Document for Bristol. In it he talked about the changes to the urban environment and how they were impacting negatively on children's play range behaviour. He was passionate in his criticism of the monotony of modern environments that offered little stimulation to children. And ten years before the Web was to take hold of children's lives, King was expressing concern about the rate of change in individual and community lives. He knew that children needed to have direct experience of the world around them if they were to fully understand it. King understood that in play children were relatively free from failure and could afford to take chances and so develop from direct experience.

> In play, the child is free from the need to produce, and may therefore experiment. In play the child is free to fantasise, because in play the child defines its own identity. In play, the child is free to change its environment, for in play the child has control. In play the child may break the rules, for in play the child makes the rules. (Frank King 1988 p. 48)[17]

A qualified youth worker, play therapist, teacher and with a masters degree in psychology, **Gordon Sturrock** (1948–) has many perspectives on childhood and playing. Of Scottish stock, he was born in India and spent part of his childhood in Brazil before returning to Scotland for his formal education. Sturrock had an equally varied career working on and supporting adventure playgrounds, running his own play equipment business, as a university tutor and as a consultant for *Creative Partnerships*, the government-funded national initiative, established to develop children's creativity and imagination. Building on this experience, Sturrock has had much to say about playwork and playing and has written over 20 papers that have been influential in playwork practice over the past 15 years. Often criticized for the 'density' of his language, Sturrock has consistently argued that playwork needs it own discrete terminology to accurately describe the exchanges adults make with children. Adding to material from his masters degree, he has argued that playwork supports children in working out – literally *playing out* – potential neuroses before they become embedded in the child's unconscious. These ideas were put forward most publicly in 1998 with 'The Colorado Paper' which brought into the public arena the following key terms: play drive or *ludido*, play cues, play returns, play frames, ludic ecology, the *metalude*, playwork containment, dysplay, play adulteration, playwork authenticity, playwork interventions.[18] Since then, these terms and concepts have been adopted by the playwork field and are now in common usage among playwork practitioners, in training materials and in the *Playwork Principles*.[19] Sturrock has generously collaborated with many key people in the UK playwork field, and that work and his contribution was celebrated in a joint Festschrift with Bob Hughes in 2007.[20]

Ken Wilber (1949–) writes about what he describes as an *integral philosophy*, which as well as philosophy covers psychology, ecology and evolution. Wilber's integral vision is based on Koestler's concept of the holon, which describes something that is both whole in itself and at the same time part of something else. Thus while human beings are also part of communities, which are part of nations, humans are also composed of organs, made up of cells, that are made up of molecules and so on. This perspective recognizes the subtle and gross influences of other concrete objects and subjective ideas on the individual. While not writing directly about play, in his writings Wilber draws together ideas from several disciplines to show that they offer complementary, rather than contradictory, perspectives. It is possible for all these views to be correct and necessary for a complete account of human existence.[21] In summary, Wilber's model shows that *human being* is both a physical and metaphysical state; that we are both objects in space and abstract ideas and that our reality is a combination of experiences from both states. The model therefore has much to say about the condition of childhood, how we experience the world and how we develop based on our experiences.

With a creative background in music and organizational change, **Pat Kane** (1964–) was the author of *The Play Ethic: A Manifesto for a Different Way of Living* (2004). In this book he states his argument that play is fundamental to both society and to the individual, and that the (protestant) work ethic that has been prominent in the West for the past 300 years is increasingly irrelevant in the twenty-first century. Using case studies from the creative worlds of musicians, artists and computer designers among others, he says 'we need to be energetic, imaginative and confident in the face of an unpredictable, contestive, emergent world'.[22] A playful attitude helps us 'maintain our adaptability, vigour and optimism in the face of an uncertain, risky and demanding world'.

While Kane's language is 'media-savvy', full of 'sound bites' and his perspective post-modern, the view he promotes is something that he could easily debate with the philosopher who started this section, Plato. They both share an appreciation of play being a state when we are most fully human and most ourselves – emotionally, cognitively, culturally and socially.

Notes

1. Given the high number of theorists written about in this section, notes are only given for specific texts or to elaborate special points. Those interested in the specific histories or papers of individuals are advised to consult the internet or a good library.

2. *Mens sana in corpore sano* – this specific phrase, usually translated as a 'healthy mind in a healthy body', comes down to us from the work of the Roman, Juvenal around 100 CE.

3. *Letters on the Aesthetic Education of Man*, Friedrich Schiller (1862).

4. Herbert Spencer (1904) *An Autobiography* London: Williams and Norgate.

5. Carl Gustav Jung (1981) *Collected Works, Vol. VI*, paras 197 and 93.

6. Johan Huizinga (1938) *Homo Ludens* London: Routledge.

7. Lev Vygotsky (1978) *Mind and Society: The Development of Higher Mental Processes* London: Harvard University Press.

8. Erik Erikson (1977) *Childhood and Society* London: Paladin.

9. Carl Rogers (1961) *On Becoming a Person: A Therapist's View of Psychotherapy* London: Constable.

10. Jerome Bruner (1966) *Toward a Theory of Instruction* Cambridge, MA: Harvard University Press.

11. Quoted in NPFA and others *Best Play* (2000), p. 6.

12. Desmond Morris (1977) *Manwatching* London: Jonathon Cape.

13. Catherine Garvey (1990) *Play – Enlarged Edition* Cambridge, MA: Harvard University Press pp. 4–5. The 1990 edition is an extended text from 1977 and includes two extra chapters on *Learning to Play* and *Play and the Real World*.

14. Brian Sutton-Smith (1997) *The Ambiguity of Play* London: Harvard University Press.

15. Brian Sutton-Smith (1988) in an article for The Association for the Study of Play, Vol. 14, No. 3. It was accessed online June 2007 from www.csuchico.edu/kine/tasp/archive/vol14no3.pdf

16. Gordon Burghardt (2005) *The Genesis of Animal Play: Testing the Limits* Cambridge, MA: MIT Press.

17. Frank King (1988) *The Right to Play – a Discussion Document of the Bristol City Council Leisure Services Committee* Bristol: Bristol City Council p. 48.

18. Gordon Sturrock and Perry Else (1998) The playground as therapeutic space: playwork as healing – known as The Colorado Paper, in *Therapeutic Playwork Reader One* (2005) Southampton: Common Threads.

19. The *Playwork Principles* establish a professional and ethical framework for playwork. Written by the Playwork Principles Scrutiny Group in 2005, they have been endorsed by Play Wales, by the Welsh Assembly Government and by SkillsActive, the national training organization for playwork.

20. A *festschrift* is a celebratory piece of writing usually offered to teachers by their students and colleagues around their sixtieth birthday. The publication in honour of Bob Hughes and Gordon Sturrock was called *Playwork Voices* and was published in 2007 by The London Centre for Playwork Education and Training.

21. This has been discussed more fully in Chapter 3 in the section on the Integral Play Framework.

22. Pat Kane (2004) *The Play Ethic: A Manifesto for a Different Way of Living* London: Macmillan p. 63.

10 The *Every Child Matters* framework in England

The *Every Child Matters* framework was set up in response to the criticism in Lord Laming's Report (2003) into the death of Victoria Climbié. In that report the link between child protection and public policy was made clear. The *Every Child Matters* Green Paper, which was to put the recommendations into action, outlined the need for integrated services which every child would use, with more targeted services for those with additional needs. The related legislation and changes to children's services set out a ten year plan that aimed to transform children's services in the years up to 2015. The legislation was designed to include all services that would have an impact on children's lives.

As part of the approach to the well-being of children and young people, the government identified five key outcomes that all children's services should work towards in support of the health and well-being of children and young people:

- being healthy: enjoying good physical and mental health and living a healthy lifestyle
- staying safe: being protected from harm and neglect and growing up able to look after themselves
- enjoying and achieving: getting the most out of life and developing broad skills for adulthood
- making a positive contribution: to the community and to society and not engaging in anti-social or offending behaviour
- economic well-being: overcoming socio-economic disadvantages to achieve their full potential in life. (Crown Copyright 2003 p. 14)[1]

The playwork sector contributed to the development of the legislation and was pleased when play was recognized as being a vital part of the children's lives. Included in the policy guidance was the need for local authorities to consider the play needs of children when constructing their local plans for children and young people. Play provision was to be included in the improvement and integration of universal services for children, with joint planning for local play spaces.

This was supported in the play sector with additional resources through the Big Lottery Fund's £155 million Children's Play initiative. Part of this money was used to support an increased infrastructure through the formal establishment of Play England, the national organization for play, to complement similar organizations in Northern Ireland, Scotland and Wales.

While this support was welcomed in the wider playwork sector, the Government made clear that any long-term support would need to be considered alongside the wider children's services network. Playwork services would therefore need to contribute to the five *Every Child Matters* outcomes.

Playwork services' contribution to the *Every Child Matters* outcomes

This section shows how playwork services might support children in their play and help meet the *Every Child Matters* outcomes. It should be stated at the outset that such an aim causes some conflict with the Playwork Principles, particularly Principle 2:

> 2 Play is a process that is freely chosen, personally directed and intrinsically motivated. That is, children and young people determine and control the content and intent of their play, by following their own instincts, ideas and interests, in their own way for their own reasons. (PPSG 2005)

The conflict arises for if children are to decide for themselves when and how they should play, the adult's influence should be minimal in that process. The play should go where it will; outcomes are not predictable, though they may be observed from activity that results. The irony is that all the recent research evidence shows that play is good for children's health and well-being, provided that the child is free to play, rather than being constrained by adult-led approaches. The challenge for settings is therefore to provide an environment that supports play that meets the child's needs and attempts to meet the five outcomes.

The following list identifies activities that adults supporting children in their play should offer to help meet the *Every Child Matters* outcomes.

The list includes the five outcomes and two additional criteria. Given that children need to be safe and healthy both physically and emotionally, those outcomes have been separated in the list below. The two additional criteria are 'led by the children' and 'the adult's role'; these recognize the approach taken by playwork practitioners when working to the Playwork Principles.

Be healthy: Emotional health

- Helping children to express their emotions and develop emotional awareness
- Supporting children to create and explore their own play experiences and enhance their own self-esteem
- Helping children to explore their own identity and the identity of others
- Showing respect to each child as a unique individual.

Be healthy: Physical health

- Providing an environment where children can be physically active indoors
- Providing a challenging outdoor environment
- Helping children be active through play.

Be safe: Emotional safety

- Creating environments and atmosphere that will help children feel emotionally safe
- Taking children's concerns seriously
- Supporting children in their right to keep themselves safe
- Ensuring that children are safe from emotional harm
- Intervening sensitively when required.

Be safe: Physical safety

- Helping children develop their own risk-taking skills
- Ensuring that children are safe from physical harm
- Intervening as necessary when a situation becomes hazardous.

Enjoy and achieve

- Supporting the child's need for new experiences
- Helping children create and achieve their own goals
- Providing an environment with opportunity for exploration, experimentation, repetition and problem solving.

Make a positive contribution

- Encouraging children to expect and show respect for themselves and others
- Facilitating working together when needed
- Sharing responsibility between children and adults.

Economic well-being

- As play is a children's right, ideally provision should meet the 'Three Frees' criteria;[2] it should be *free* to access, activities should be *freely* chosen by the children and they should be *free* to leave when they wish. This will create difficulties for play provision that offers a care service, however the criteria are in line with the ethos of the Playwork Principles.

Led by the children

- Giving children choices for most aspects of their play
- Encouraging children to make decisions about their own play
- Involving children in creating rules where they are needed.

The adult's role

- Applying the Playwork Principles to practise
- Using experiential and reflective teamwork skills to create a good team that supports play
- Using leadership skills within a playwork ethos to lead the team.

Play should always follow the children's lead and so the list gives an indication of the types of support that could be offered. The list is not intended to be prescriptive and indicates possible activities rather than a curriculum for play.

Notes

1. Crown Copyright (2003) *Every Child Matters Green Paper* Norwich: HMSO p. 14.
2. The Three Frees criteria were first formulated by the author in 2006 as part of work supporting the development of play indicators.

Appendix

Playwork Principles 2005

These Principles establish the professional and ethical framework for playwork and as such must be regarded as a whole. They describe what is unique about play and playwork, and provide the playwork perspective for working with children and young people. They are based on the recognition that children and young people's capacity for positive development will be enhanced if given access to the broadest range of environments and play opportunities.

1 All children and young people need to play. The impulse to play is innate. Play is a biological, psychological and social necessity, and is fundamental to the healthy development and well-being of individuals and communities.

2 Play is a process that is freely chosen, personally directed and intrinsically motivated. That is, children and young people determine and control the content and intent of their play, by following their own instincts, ideas and interests, in their own way for their own reasons.

3 The prime focus and essence of playwork is to support and facilitate the play process and this should inform the development of play policy, strategy, training and education.

4 For playworkers, the play process takes precedence and playworkers act as advocates for play when engaging with adult-led agendas.

5 The role of the playworker is to support all children and young people in the creation of a space in which they can play.

6 The playworker's response to children and young people playing is based on a sound up-to-date knowledge of the play process, and reflective practice.

7 Playworkers recognize their own impact on the play space and also the impact of children and young people's play on the playworker.

8 Playworkers choose an intervention style that enables children and young people to extend their play. All playworker intervention must balance risk with the developmental benefit and well-being of children.

Playwork Principles Scrutiny Group, Cardiff 2005

References

AA Motoring Trust (2003) accessed 5 May 2007 from www.theaa.com/public_affairs/reports/facts_about_road_accidents_and_children.pdf

Bailey D (2005) *Bailey's Democracy* London: Thames and Hudson

Bateson G (1973) *Steps to an Ecology of Mind* London: Granada Publishing

Batty D (2005) 'Timeline: a history of child protection' *The Guardian* Wednesday 18 May, 2005

BBC4 (6 June 2008) *A Revolution in Childhood*

Berne E (1964) *Games People Play* London: Penguin Books

Biddolph S (1997) *Raising Boys* London: Thorsons

Bruner J (1966) *Toward a Theory of Instruction* Cambridge, MA: Harvard University Press

Burghardt G (2005) *The Genesis of Animal Play: Testing the Limits* Cambridge, MA: MIT Press

Cawson P, Wattam C, Brooker S and Kelly G (2000) *Child Maltreatment in the UK: A Study of the Prevalence of Child Abuse and Neglect* London, NSPCC [Online] accessed 5 May 2007 from www.nspcc.org.uk/Inform/research/Findings

Chief Medical Officer (2003) *Health Check: On the State of Public Health* London: Department of Health

Cobb E (1977) *The Ecology of Imagination in Childhood* Dallas: Spring Publications

Cole-Hamilton I, Harrop A and Street C (2002) *Making the Case for Play – Gathering the Evidence* London: National Children's Bureau

Crown Copyright (2003) *Every Child Matters Green Paper* Norwich: HMSO

Csikszentmihalyi M (1990) *Flow – The Psychology of Optimal Experience* New York: Harper and Row

Czuky M (Ed.) (1979) *How Does It feel?* London: Thames and Hudson

Danks F and Schofield J (2005) *Nature's Playground* London: Frances Lincoln Ltd.

Dawkins R (1989) *The Selfish Gene* Oxford: Oxford University Press

Eno B (1994) *A Year with Swollen Appendices* London: Faber and Faber

Erikson E (1977) *Childhood and Society* London: Paladin

Flemmen A (2005) 'Real play: a recognized sensory-motor behaviour in Norway' *Playrights*, 26 (4) IPA

Frost JL, Wortham SC and Reifel S (2008) *Play and Child Development* Upper Saddle River: Pearson Education Inc.

Fulghum R (1991) *Uh-Oh some Observations from Both Sides of the Refrigerator Door* New York: Ivy Books

Garvey C (1990) *Play* Cambridge, MA: Harvard University Press

Ghiselin B (1952) *The Creative Process* Berkeley: University of California Press

Gill T (2007) *No Fear: Growing up in a Risk-Averse Society* London: Gulbenkian

Goldschmied E and Jackson S (1994) *People under Three: Young Children in Day Care* London: Routledge

Goleman D (1996) *Emotional Intelligence* London: Bloomsbury

Gopnik A, Meltzoff AN and Kuhl P (1999) *How Babies Think: The Science of Childhood* London: Weidenfield and Nicholson

Gordon G (2003) 'Play: the movement of love' *EarthLight Magazine No48*, 13 (3) accessed from www.earthlight.org/2003/essay48_gordon.html

Gussin Paley V (2004) *A Child's Work: The Importance of Fantasy Play* London: University of Chicago Press

Hart R (1992) *Children's Participation: From Tokenism to Citizenship Innocenti Essay 4* Florence: UNICEF International Child Development Centre

Health & Safety Executive Report 426, 2002 Playgrounds – Risks, Benefits and Choices (2002)

Holland P (2003) *We Don't Play with Guns Here: War, Weapon and Superhero Play in the Early Years* Maidenhead: Open University Press

Hughes B (1996a) *A Playworker's Taxonomy of Play Types* London: Playlink

Hughes B (1996b) *Play Environments: A Question of Quality* London: Playlink

Hughes B (2001) *Evolutionary Playwork and Reflective Analytic Practice* London: Routledge

Hughes B (2006) *Play Types – Speculations and Possibilities* London: London Centre for Playwork Education and Training

Huizinga J (1938) *Homo Ludens* London: Routledge

Johnson MH (2008) Brain development in childhood: A literature review and synthesis for the Byron Review on the impact of new technologies on children. Accessed from www.dfes.gov.uk/byronreview/

Jung CG (1981) *Collected Works* Vol. VI Princeton, NJ: Bollingen

Kamen T (2005) *The Playworker's Handbook* London: Hodder Arnold

Kane P (2004) *The Play Ethic: A Manifesto for a Different Way of Living* London: Macmillan

King F (1988) *The Right to Play – a Discussion Document of the Bristol City Council* Leisure Services Committee Bristol: Bristol City Council

Lee A, Carter JA and Ping X (1995) 'Children's conceptions of ability in physical education' *Journal of Teaching Physical Education,* 14 (4) 384–393

Lester S and Russell W (2008a) *Play for a Change, Summary Briefing* London: National Children's Bureau

Lester S and Russell W (2008b) *Play for a Change, Full Report* London: National Children's Bureau

Lewis CS (2004) *Chronicles of Narnia* London: Harper Collins

Lindon J (2001) *Understanding Children's Play* Cheltenham: Nelson Thornes Ltd.

Mackett R (2004) *Making Children's Lives More Active* University College London: Centre for Transport Studies

McKendrick J (2000) 'The dangers of safe play Children 5–16' Research Briefing No. 22, Economic and Social Research Council

Miller J (1997) *Never Too Young* London: National Early Years Network

Morris D (1977) *Manwatching* London: Jonathon Cape

Morris D (2005) *Bailey's Democracy* London: Thames and Hudson

National Playing Fields Association/Children's Play Council/Playlink (2000) *Best Play* London: NPFA

Nicholson S (1971) 'How not to cheat children: the theory of loose parts' *Landscape Architecture Quarterly*, 62 (1) 30–34

Nutbrown C (Ed.) (1996) *Respectful Educators – Capable Learners* London: Paul Chapman

Opie I and Opie P (1959) *The Lore and Language of Schoolchildren* Oxford: Oxford University Press

Paoletti J (no date) *Dressing for sexes* online accessed 12 July 2008 from www.gentlebirth.org/archives/pinkblue.html

Peter L (1977) *Quotations for Our Time* London: Souvenir Press

Play Safety Forum (2002) *Managing Risk in Play Provision: A Position Statement* London: Children's Play Council

Playlink (2001) *Making Sense: Playwork in Practice* London: Playlink

Pringle A (2004) 'Can watching football be a component of developing a state of mental health for men?' *The Journal of the Royal Society for the Promotion of Health*, 124 (3) 122–128

Rideout VJ, Vandewater EA and Wartella EA (2003) 'Zero to Six: Electronic Media in the Lives of Infants, Toddlers and Preschoolers' Kaiser Family Foundation Report. 28 October. Quoted in *The Biologist*, 54 (1), February 2007

Rogers C (1961) *On Becoming a Person: A Therapist's View of Psychotherapy* London: Constable

Roopnarine JL (Ed.) (2003) *Play and Educational Theory and Practice, Play and Culture Studies Vol. 5* Westport, CT: Praeger

Rowan D (21 May 2005) 'Have children really forgotten how to play?' *The Times Magazine* online accessed 11 June 2007 from www.davidrowan.com

Russell W and Nottingham City Council (2006) *Reframing Playwork; Reframing Challenging Behaviour* Nottingham City Council

Smilansky S (1968) *The Effects of Sociodramatic Play on Disadvantaged Preschool Children* New York: Wiley

Spencer H (1904) *An Autobiography* London: Williams and Norgate

Sturrock G and Else P (1998) *Therapeutic Playwork Reader One* (2005) Southampton: Common Threads

Sutton-Smith B (1988) *The Association for the Study of Play*, Vol. 14, No. 3 accessed on line June 2007 from www.csuchico.edu/kine/tasp/archive/vol14no3.pdf

Sutton-Smith B (1997) *The Ambiguity of Play* London: Harvard University Press

Sutton-Smith B (2003) 'Play as a parody of emotional vulnerability', in Roopnarine JL (Ed.) *Play and Educational Theory and Practice, Play and Culture Studies Vol. 5* Westport, CT: Praeger

Swimme B (2001) *The Universe is a Green Dragon* Rochester: Bear and Co.

Thorne B (1993) *Gender Play – Girls and Boys in School* Buckingham: Open University Press

Tulley G (2007) *5 Dangerous Things You Should Let Your Kids Do* accessed from www.ted.com

Vygotsky L (1933) *Play and Its Role in the Mental Development of the Child* accessed from www.marxists.org/archive/vygotsky/works/1933/play.htm

Vygotsky L (1978) *Mind and Society: The Development of Higher Mental Processes* London: Harvard University Press

Wardle J, Henning Brodersen N, Cole T, Jarvis M and Boniface D (2006) 'Development of adiposity in adolescence' *British Medical Journal*, (332) 1130–1135

Wheway R (2007) *Urban Myths about Children's Playgrounds* London: Child Accident Prevention Trust

Wheway R and Millward A (1997) *Child's Play Facilitating Play on Housing Estates* London: Chartered Institute of Housing/Joseph Rowntree Foundation

Wilber K (1991) *Grace and Grit* Dublin: Newleaf

Wilber K (2000) *Integral Psychology* Boston: Shambhala

Wilson EO (1986) *Biophilia* Boston: Harvard University Press

Winnicott DW (1971) *Playing and Reality* London: Penguin

Winston R (2002) *Human Instinct* London: Bantam Press

Index